DEVELOPING LEISURE TIME SKILLS FOR PERSONS WITH AUTISM

A PRACTICAL APPROACH FOR HOME, SCHOOL AND COMMUNIT

Phyllis Coyne
Colleen Nyberg
Mary Lou Vandenburg

Future Horizons, Inc.

FUTURE HORIZONS INC.

Future Horizons, Inc.
720 N. Fielder Rd.
Arlington, TX 76012

800-489-0727 • 817-277-0727
817-277-2270 fax

www.futurehorizons-autism.net - Website
edfuture@onramp.net - email

All rights reserved. Original purchaser is authorized to re reproduce individual cards and blanks (assessment and training) forms for classroom use only without special permission from publisher. However, reproduction or republication of this book as a whole is strictly prohibited.

Activity Cards Illustrations by Kevin Wollenwebber
Edited by Glenn Williams
Page Design by Anita Jones

© 1999 Future Horizons, Inc.
ISBN 1-885477-56-2

Contents

Acknowledgments i

Introduction iii

Chapter 1 **Leisure and Autism** 1
    Description of Three Individuals 2
    The Importance of Developing Competencies for Leisure 3
    Leisure Materials and Activities for Individuals with Autism .. 4
    Summary 5

Chapter 2 **Components of Leisure Development** 7
    The Immediate Component 9
    The Exposure Component 10
    The Training Component 11
    Interrelationship of the Components of Leisure Development ... 12

Chapter 3 **Leisure Assessment and Selection** 13
    Assessing the Leisure Patterns and Skills of the Individual .. 14
    Assessing the Leisure Preferences of the Individual 21
    Assessing the Leisure Preferences of Family & Friends 22
    Selection of Leisure Materials and Activities 27
    Summary 31

Chapter 4 **The Immediate Component of Leisure Development** 33
    Key Elements of the Immediate Component 33
    Meaningful Occupation of Unstructured Time 34
    Untrained Activities with Minimal Supervision 34
    Sensory Preferences 35
    Self Determined Use 39
    Age Appropriate Materials 39
    Ongoing Assessment 39
    Summary 40

Chapter 5 **The Exposure Component of Leisure Development** 41
    Key Elements of the Exposure Component 41
    A Systematic, Structured Approach 41
    Minimal Training with Multiple Exposure 42
    The Preferences of Individual, Family & Friends 42
    Trainer-directed Exposure 43
    Age Appropriate Materials and Activities 43

Ongoing Assessment 44
The Activity Cards 44
Activity Assessment Card 48
Summary 50

Chapter 6   **The Training Component of Leisure Development** 51
Key Elements of the Training Component 51
Leisure Activities and Related Skills Development 51
Ongoing Training 56
Preferences of Individuals, Family and Friends 60
Individualized Program 62
Community Referenced Activities 65
Ongoing Assessment 65
Summary 65

Appendices 67
A. Typical Leisure Behavior & Age-Appropriate Activities Lists 69
B. Directions & Forms for Leisure Assessment 79
C. Activity Cards 91
D. Discrepancy Analysis with Hypothesis Form 221

References 225

Acknowledgments

We wish to thank our friends and family members who have supported us through the challenge of writing this book.

A number of individuals and agencies have been instrumental in the development of these materials. It is impossible to thank them all. We wish to thank all the parents of children with autism and the children themselves, who have provided the impetus for the development of this book. We wish to extend a special thanks to the families who participated in testing these materials.

Jan Janzen, former Oregon Department of Education Statewide Autism Specialist, and author of *Understanding the Nature of Autism*, as well as Columbia Regional Program—Autism Services provided us with a solid foundation in autism and encouraged us to develop an approach to assist individuals with autism in their leisure. Dr. Steve Brannon, Professor Emeritus in Special Education at Portland State University and longtime supporter of leisure education for individuals with special needs, provided thoughtful comments during the creation of the Components of Leisure Development. Kathy Henley, founder of the Autistic Children's Activity Program (ACAP), provided a catalyst for the development of the Activity Cards.

Introduction

Leisure represents free time, when an individual can choose to pursue activities of interest. For most of us, leisure is enjoyable and something that we eagerly anticipate. We may choose to use leisure time to challenge ourselves, to relax, to express ourselves creatively, to be entertained, or to socialize.

For the individual with autism, and for his or her family, unstructured or free time may be one of the most challenging times. The families of individuals with autism generally do not look forward to going to the zoo or to an evening at home playing table games. Parents of young children with autism often wish that their child could entertain himself or herself appropriately, even for just a few minutes. Teachers and others working with individuals with autism want to know how to assist them to be more independent and self-directing in leisure. Both parents and professionals have remarked that when individuals with autism are doing things that they like and that make sense to them, problem behavior often decreases. Developing competence in leisure is a positive means of reducing inappropriate self-stimulation or stereotypic behavior. It increases enjoyment for all.

The purpose of this book is to provide a comprehensive, structured approach for individuals with autism to develop leisure interests and skills for school, home and community. It provides practical information and guidelines to enable individuals with autism to develop competencies for choosing and engaging in enjoyable leisure activities. Parents, other caregivers and professionals will find the materials easy to use.

This book is unique in the manner in which it considers the personal preferences of individuals with autism and moves them toward more meaningful and enjoyable leisure. It capitalizes on the individual with autism's strengths in visual-spatial manipulation and establishing routines, and uses their interest in sensory feedback.

The approach in this book has three major components:
1) providing materials that generate immediate interest by means of their sensory properties
2) providing structured, repeated exposure to new activities to develop interests
3) providing training in the skills necessary for choosing and participating in preferred activities in the home, school/work and community.

These components were developed to be part of a comprehensive approach, but are not meant to be implemented sequentially. The activities and components involved will depend on the unique needs and interests of the individual.

The material in this book can be used effectively with individuals of varying ages and severity of autism. It is designed to be individualized to fit personal interests and needs. Several appendices of resources, including blank forms, Activity Cards, and references, assist the reader to further individualize the plan.

To assist individuals with autism to develop competencies in leisure, it is necessary for parents, other caregivers and professionals to work as a team. This book provides practical suggestions that can be utilized by a variety of people who know individuals with autism. Most of the elements can be implemented by anyone interested in helping individuals with autism, regardless of their experience level. For instance, the Activity Cards were designed to be used by parents, baby-sitters, respite care providers or any others who interact with the individual during unstructured time. Some of the more technical aspects of assessment and training may be best facilitated by professionals, such as therapeutic recreation specialists and other recreation professionals, special educators, other education professionals, or residential trainers.

The authors have each worked in the field of autism for over fifteen years. This experience, along with backgrounds in therapeutic recreation, special education, regular education, and psychology, provide the foundation for the development of concepts and approaches presented in this book. We hope you find them useful.

Chapter 1

Leisure and Autism

Leisure provides freedom to engage in preferred activities of one's own choosing. We are all different in our leisure pursuits. Some of us like doing things primarily by ourselves and some of us are more group-oriented. However, most of us do a variety of activities alone and with others in our home and community. Most of us have learned activities by watching or participating with family and friends. Some of us have learned other activities through classes, clubs, or by reading instructions. For most of us, leisure/play behaviors and interests develop in a predictable manner. This pattern of development is well illustrated in the Typical Leisure/Play Behaviors and Interests List located in Appendix A.

There is a wide range of severity among individuals with autism. Autism may also be accompanied by other disabilities. Yet despite these individual differences, the nature of autism generally inhibits the development of leisure interests and skills. Individuals with autism seldom learn through informal observation or through imitation of their friends and families. They develop leisure/play behaviors and interests in their own way. During free time, they often establish their own routines. They may use the same materials repetitively for a long period of time. They often do not show interest or play with objects in the same manner as other children. They may not understand the intended use or purpose of leisure materials. Instead, the materials may be used primarily for their sensory qualities. If they learn to interact appropriately with a certain toy, person, or place, they may not be able to generalize this skill to other toys, persons or places. Without assistance, they are unlikely to explore new leisure options or to feel comfortable in new activities.

Individuals with autism can learn to develop leisure interests and skills that they can choose and enjoy in unstructured time. To develop their interests and skills, they need a comprehensive, structured approach. Their interest in visual-spatial manipulation, in establishing routines and in sensory feedback can all be used positively to develop leisure competence. The methods of leisure assessment and the Components of Leisure Development presented in this book provide a comprehensive, structured approach that considers the unique needs of the individual with autism.

Description of Three Individuals

Although individuals with autism share common characteristics, they are unique individuals. The following depicts three individuals of different ages and severity of autism before they were involved with the Components of Leisure Development. These three individuals will be referred to throughout this book to illustrate this approach.

Case 1: Dan

Dan is a handsome 17 year old student with both autism and a vision impairment. He attends his neighborhood high school. His autism causes inconsistent results in both vision and cognitive testing, so the degree of his vision and cognitive impairments are difficult to assess. Although much of his speech is echolalic, he communicates basic requests to people he knows verbally and uses a pictorial request system in the community. He is well-liked by his peers and educational staff.

Dan has a limited number of things that he enjoys doing in unstructured time. He has always enjoyed manipulating his environment by making loud sounds and altering lighting. One of the ways in which he has made sounds at school is to break the glass on the fire alarm. At home, he put out all the lights in the house by throwing objects at the light bulbs. He enjoys recording voices of favorite people and listening to them over and over. He also enjoys the feeling of warm air and likes to lie on heat vents. When not supervised, he may gorge on food. Because he enjoys jumping and other vestibular activities, his grandfather designed and constructed a whirling ride that Dan can use privately in his basement.

He lives with his mother. They enjoy listening to music together. His mother pays some same-age peers to do afterschool activities with Dan while she is at work.

Case 2: Julie

Julie is an eleven year old girl who primarily uses verbal language to communicate. She attends her local school and is included in a general education fifth grade class. She spends one hour a day in the resource room. She relies on a written schedule to make the transition from one activity to another and written instructions to complete a sequence of tasks. Julie's sensory preference is visual, but she tolerates some auditory input. She has difficulty with tactile input.

At this time, Julie's preferred leisure activity is using electronic games, such as Nintendo or Game Boy. At school, she chooses one of them during free time. If they are not available, she either does nothing or prefers to play alone. At home, she would play electronic games all the time, if it were allowed.

Case 3: John

John is an engaging, energetic four year old with autism. He attends the local early childhood special education program. In addition, his mother takes him to an indoor playground at a nearby church basement. Communication is difficult for John. He makes requests in unusual ways, such as by reaching, grabbing or otherwise retrieving his items. He protests by screaming, hitting, and kicking. He has recently begun to understand the order of his world through picture sequences. However, he does not understand the power that pictures might have in getting him what he wants.

Activities that John prefers are swinging, rocking, bouncing and jumping. He is rough with any object. He likes to explore how objects sound or look when they are bounced on the floor. Both breakable objects and rubber balls are indiscriminately dropped on the floor. Music can be very soothing for John and is usually used at night to help him sleep. Soft, cuddly objects upset him, but he likes hard plastic objects, especially a plastic phone. He uses the phone in a variety of ways, including banging it on himself and bouncing it on the floor. John lives with his mother, father and older sister.

The Importance of Developing Competencies for Leisure

When taught to enjoy their free time by engaging in personally satisfying, age-appropriate leisure activities, individuals with autism experience many benefits. Leisure skills can replace challenging behaviors that previously provided sensory stimulation. Being able to appropriately entertain oneself during free time can reduce the stress of having an individual with autism in the home or community.

Leisure skills and interests can also create opportunities for social interaction with peers. Individuals with autism may find friendships through leisure pursuits and common interests. For instance, one higher-functioning young man found friends through a computer club at which everyone wanted to talk about his favorite topic, computers.

Of course, personal enjoyment is the primary benefit of having leisure skills and is an end in itself.

Leisure Materials and Activities for Individuals with Autism

There are no "autistic" toys, games or activities. Given appropriate exposure, individuals with autism often find fun where other people find fun. They need to be exposed to a wide variety of experiences and activities to develop broader interests. Like all of us, interests change over time and an individual may later prefer something that was initially of little interest.

By definition, leisure is a time to participate in things that one likes to do. Despite personal differences in individuals with autism, some specific qualities may make leisure materials and activities more meaningful and successful. These qualities include materials and activities that are understandable, reactive, comfortable, active and visual-spatial.

Understandable

Individuals with autism often have difficulty understanding an activity, the purpose of leisure materials or what to do with them. Some properties that can make materials and activities more understandable are:
1) clear, static rules
2) a well-defined beginning and end
3) a predictable or repetitive quality
4) a clear visual representation of what to do
5) the need for minimal verbal direction
6) structure

Reactive

Reactive leisure materials provide reinforcement through sensory feedback. When a reactive material is acted upon, something clearly happens and it looks different. Good reactive leisure materials provide lights, sounds, movements and tactile sensation strong enough to promote interest. Research results indicate that play activity in children with autism is stimulated by the use of reactive toys. In comparison to non-reactive toys, the reactive toys had substantially greater influence on the amount of time each child engaged in toy manipulation. A number of individuals with autism are attracted to electronic and computer games, in part, because of their reactive features. Visually stimulating objects and music often generate interest for the same reasons.

Consideration needs to be given to individual preferences for sensory feedback and the intensity of sensory stimulation desired. This will be addressed in more depth in later chapters. A list of sample leisure materials which provide sensory feedback is included in Chapter 4.

<u>Comfortable</u>

The previously discussed features will help to make materials or an activity more comfortable for the individual. Other qualities to increase the level of comfort include that the activities or materials be:
1) challenging, without being over stimulating
2) within the individual's ability level
3) limited in their demands for complex social interaction
4) offering the opportunity for a sense of control or mastery

<u>Active</u>

Some individuals with autism may stay in one place for prolonged periods of time doing a highly preferred activity. However, as a general rule, it is important to avoid activities that require staying in one place for a long time. For instance, some table games not only go for a long time, they may require a significant wait between turns.

Young children, in particular, need some activities that involve gross motor skills, such as climbing, for physical release. Rhythmic activities, like swinging or swimming, are often enjoyed by individuals with autism.

<u>Visual-Spatial</u>

Additional characteristics of motivating leisure activities include the repetitive manipulation of objects, putting things in order, or fitting objects into spaces. A number of individuals with autism may like to do puzzles, because puzzles have understandable features. Puzzles also have concrete pieces, rather than imaginary ones, for physical manipulation.

Summary

The nature of autism generally limits the development of leisure interests and skills. Individuals with autism seldom learn through informal observation or through imitation. They develop their own unique patterns. Individuals with autism can develop leisure interests and skills that they can choose and enjoy through a comprehensive, structured approach. Their interest in visual-spatial manipulation, establishing routines and sensory feedback can all be used positively to develop leisure competence. Without extra assistance and structure, they are unlikely to understand or learn leisure activities.

Individuals with autism need to be exposed, in a structured manner, to a wide variety of experiences and activities to develop broader interests. Some features of meaningful and successful leisure materials and activities are that they are understandable, reactive, comfortable, active, and spatially manipulative.

Chapter 2
Components of Leisure Development

Many programs that claim to prepare individuals with autism for leisure lack a systematic approach to develop interests and skills. Even in instructional settings such as schools, recreation and play are often relegated to less structured aspects of the curriculum.

This book provides a comprehensive, systematic approach to develop leisure skills and interests in the home, school/work and community. As previously mentioned, it presents practical guidelines for three critical Components of Leisure Development for individuals with autism:
1) using untrained activities with sensory features that provide immediate meaningful occupation of unstructured time (*the Immediate Component*)
2) systematic, structured exposure to leisure activities that develop potential interests (*the Exposure Component*)
3) training in leisure activity and related skills to develop independent choice-making and participation in activities of interest (*the Training Component*).

Each component utilizes age-appropriate activities of interest to the individual and utilizes ongoing assessment to make necessary changes in how and what activities are provided. Because each Component has a different purpose and goal, each differs in the amount of training and direction provided.

The table illustrating the Components of Leisure Development provides a conceptualization of the necessary elements required in the development of meaningful leisure participation that is presented in this book. Although all people need these elements to develop their leisure lifestyle, individuals with autism need more systematic, planned experiences with each Component.

Components of Leisure Development

Immediate	Exposure	Training
Key Elements:	**Key Elements:**	**Key Elements:**
• Meaningful occupation of unstructured time of activities	• Systematic structured approach to exploration	• Leisure activity and related skill development
• Untrained activities with minimal supervision	• Minimal training with multiple exposures	• Ongoing training
• Based on sensory preferences	• Preferences of individual, family and friends	• Preferences of individual, family and friends
• Self-determined use	• Trainer directed	• Individualized program
• Age appropriate materials	• Age appropriate	• Community referenced
• Ongoing assessment	• Ongoing assessment	• Ongoing assessment

The Immediate Component

The purpose of the *Immediate Component* is to provide materials that will generate interest and use for short periods during unstructured time. It provides immediate, meaningful occupation of time with highly reinforcing materials that are based on sensory preferences. This component may offer relief from the constant supervision needed by many individuals with autism who lack leisure interests and skills.

Parents have indicated that the inability of their children with autism to entertain themselves appropriately and to cope with unstructured time is a major problem. Many parents wish their child could be appropriately self-occupied with minimal supervision for even five minutes while they set the table. Therefore, there is a strong need for materials that the young person would be motivated to use and that could be used safely after it is demonstrated to him or her.

To meet this need, the authors have identified age-appropriate materials that are available in local stores and can meaningfully occupy free time with minimal supervision. Since individuals with autism show more interest and interact more with materials that provide sensory feedback, all materials chosen provide some form of sensory feedback.

Leisure materials which have sensory properties that are enjoyed by the individual, and are similar or incompatible to problem behaviors, can reduce unusual behaviors and provide individuals with a more acceptable means to independently occupy their free time. When the materials are portable, they can be used for enjoyment in former trouble areas, such as waiting for the bus or at the doctor's office, as well as at identified free time. This Component has potential application for unstructured times in all settings — home, school/work, and community — and with all ages of individuals of autism.

This Component is described in fuller detail in Chapter 4. It is particularly useful in the home and during unstructured times in the community. Although it is unlikely to be an IEP or IFSP objective, the use of immediate leisure materials might be an important accommodation or initial strategy in an educational setting.

The Exposure Component

The purpose of the *Exposure Component* is to develop awareness of, and interest in, recreation activities for future training. To become aware of the wide range of options available for leisure, one needs information about activities as well as exposure to these options. Most children learn about leisure opportunities through their family, friends, school groups, or the media.

Many individuals with autism do not have a variety of interests. It is often difficult, at first, to find activities of interest to them. Many will initially resist activities, because they are new and they do not understand them. Initially few activities may result in pleasurable responses. However, individuals with autism will often learn to enjoy new activities through the structure and repetition of the Exposure Component.

For a person to determine whether an activity would be meaningful and enjoyable, both information about the activity and an opportunity to experience it are necessary. Due to their difficulty with new situations and activities, many individuals with autism are not exposed to the range of leisure opportunities available to their peers. Therefore, a systematic, structured approach to exploration and exposure needs to be provided.

A range of materials and opportunities need to be provided over time to help determine what the individual with autism might enjoy. Since individuals with autism may be reluctant with new activities or have difficulty understanding them, it is important to provide multiple opportunities to experience each activity before trying to determine if an activity would be meaningful and enjoyable for the individual. This exposure needs to be structured and carefully directed by the trainer so that the individual can experience what it is like to appropriately engage in the activity. It is important to remember that interests change over time and that an individual may like something better later on in life.

Chapter 5 describes this Component in detail. It also provides directions and specific teaching tips for a variety of activities in a user-friendly Activity Card format. The Activity Cards in Appendix C can be used by a variety of people at home, school/work, and the community. They can be readily used at home by a parent or babysitter. They can also be used in a school setting to prepare for and structure field trips and special classes, such as art. Day program and residential facilities staff will also find them useful in structuring leisure time.

The Training Component

The purpose of the *Training Component* is to develop the necessary activity and activity-related skills which will allow the individual to participate in enjoyed activities, in natural settings, with preferred friends and family. In addition to the skills required to do the activity itself, it includes an awareness of leisure and free time, an identification of community and personal resources, choice-making skills, the ability to self-initiate activities, social interaction skills, and problem-solving skills.

Generally, people learn leisure activities and related leisure skills from friends or family members, through classes, clubs or organizations, or by reading. It may involve informal training (such as, imitating what another person does) or formal instruction (such as, taking a class). Due to the limited ability of many individuals with autism to model behavior, systematic instruction is needed. Their difficulty with incidental learning and generalization makes it vital to teach related skills for each activity.

Instruction must be individualized for the student by using educational best practices. In Chapter 6, procedures are provided to assist in individualizing and designing leisure training, based on the needs of individuals with autism. Blank forms are provided in the Appendices, in addition to the sample completed forms within the chapter. This Component is designed to be used in instructional settings and assumes some knowledge of instructional techniques for those with autism. It is best facilitated by professionals whose role is to train for leisure development.

Interrelationship of the Components of Leisure Development

Like all of us, the leisure pursuits and interests of individuals with autism change over time. We may try new things to see if we like them. If we like an activity, we may purposefully develop skills in it. Although the Components of Leisure Development are presented separately, they are not designed to be offered in a sequence. It is assumed that the Components will be used, based on the unique and changing needs and interests of the individual with autism.

The initial focus will be the *Immediate Component* for individuals who cannot safely occupy themselves for even short periods of time. The focus at some point will be assessing and developing leisure interests through the *Exposure Component*. At another point in time, the individual may be engaged in the *Training Component* in the leisure activity and related skills for an activity and still need the type of portable leisure materials that provide sensory feedback addressed in the *Immediate Component*.

All the Components may be part of a person's leisure lifestyle development. For instance, a middle school student's leisure might include:
1) playing with a hand-held game (*the Immediate Component*)
2) being exposed to new activities through art or other elective classes at school, or through neighborhood friends, or through a youth organization like the Girl Scouts (*the Exposure Component*)
3) taking classes through the Park Bureau's community centers or community schools (*the Training Component*).

When an individual's present leisure lifestyle is examined, it may become apparent that further development in a particular area is needed. An individual who is not meaningfully self-occupied for even five minutes needs *Immediate* leisure materials and *Exposure* to potential activities of interest to access preferences. An individual for whom interests have been identified needs *Training* in the activity and related skills. Similarly an individual who has independent activity participation skills, but cannot independently initiate or prepare for the activity needs further *Training*. An individual who has few activities s/he does independently at home, in the community, and at school might need further *Exposure* to develop further interests or training to do presently enjoyed activities in other settings with other people.

The use of the Components of Leisure Development must be individualized for the unique needs and interests of the person with autism. Assessment of the individual's present interests and functioning in leisure is critical to the choice of *Immediate* leisure materials, *Exposure* and *Training* that are appropriate for the individual. Chapter 3: Leisure Assessment and Selection provides a framework for developing the necessary information for decision making.

Chapter 3
Leisure Assessment and Selection

Before identifying leisure activities and materials, it is important to assess the individual's present leisure pattern and competencies, as well as the leisure interests of the individual, family and friends. Leisure assessment is critical to the selection of leisure materials and activities that relate to the unique needs and interests of the individual. It provides the foundation for making decisions about leisure development. Leisure assessment will save time and frustration for both individuals with autism and the people who are concerned about their leisure development.

This chapter provides samples of completed assessment forms; blank assessment forms are located in Appendix B. Three individuals with autism were introduced in Chapter 1: Dan, Julie and John. Dan, our high school student, will be used to illustrate what the assessment might look like for one individual.

The Leisure assessment presented in this chapter requires participation by those who know the individual with autism the best. It both precedes use of the Components of Leisure Development and is an ongoing process that provides feedback on the development of leisure competencies.

Leisure Assessment does not need to be complicated. Sometimes the individual's leisure pattern and interests are already known, and may be easily recorded on a summary profile. The summary profile can then be updated as further interests and skills develop. However, the interests and skills of other individuals with autism will be less obvious and require more formal assessment. If the initial focus of leisure development is the *Immediate Component*, it may be adequate to begin by assessing sensory preferences. If the individual is to be involved in the *Exposure* or *Training Components*, it is important to know more about the individual's leisure interests and skills. The ongoing assessment during the *Immediate, Exposure* and *Training Components* will provide valuable information about the individual's interests, as well as the degree of support needed. It provides vital information to use in modifying the goals and strategies for leisure development.

There are many ways that an individual's leisure competence and interests can be assessed. The reader is encouraged to select the methods that are most useful in individual situations. The forms of assessment discussed in this chapter will meet different needs for initial information and for ongoing assessment. They include: a summary profile, interviews, direct observation, and questionnaires. Dan's case will be used to illustrate the use of each form throughout this chapter.

Assessing the Leisure Pattern and Skills of the Individual

<u>Leisure Lifestyle Profile</u>

The Leisure Lifestyle Profile is presented first because it is an effective summary profile for planning individualized leisure development and to monitor progress during the *Immediate, Exposure* and *Training Components*. It offers an overview of the individual's present leisure pattern and skills. This summary profile is a valuable tool in tracking leisure development. Information from the interviews and observation described in this chapter, along with ongoing assessment, can be consolidated on this form.

The Leisure Lifestyle Profile is comprised of six grids that represent the environment and social interaction in leisure activities. These grids include:
1) home alone
2) home with others
3) community alone
4) community with others
5) school/work alone
6) school/work with others.

Activities that the individual does for a minimum of fifteen minutes, at least twelve times a year, are identified and listed in the appropriate grids.

Seven columns correspond to the leisure activity and related skills for leisure participation. These leisure and related skills are further described in Chapter 6. They include: awareness of leisure and free time, identification of community and personal resources, choice-making, self-initiation of activities, activity skills, social interaction skills, and problem-solving skills.

The following provides the abbreviations and meanings used for each of these columns.
    ID Time: Identification of free time for engaging in preferred activities.
    Resources: Identification and utilization of necessary equipment, attire, money and resources for activity.
    Choice: Selection of activity.
    Initiate: Self-initiation of the activity.
    Skills: Demonstration of skills necessary for participation in the activity.
    Interact: Demonstration of social interaction skills required for the activity.
    Problem Solve: Demonstration of problem-solving skills related to participation in the activity.

An individual's success in leisure is dependent less on how many skills are mastered than on their independence in performing the skills. The individual's present level of functioning for each activity is indicated in the columns for the leisure and related skills using the following code:

- **I** = Independently completes the activity without cue or prompt
- **E** = Emerging; knows what the activity is about or can partially do it without adaptations
- **PP** = Partially participates in the activity with certain adaptations at a predetermined level
- **TA** = Total assistance needed to complete the activity
- **NA** = Not applicable; not required in the activity or an unconventional activity in which the skill is not defined.

The comments section allows for any special notation, such as adaptations or supports needed. A blank Leisure Lifestyle Profile form can be found in Appendix B.

The Profile gives an overall picture of the balance of activities in different settings. An example of a completed Leisure Lifestyle Profile follows. It reflects Dan's leisure pattern and skills before application of the Components of Leisure Development.

LEISURE LIFESTYLE PROFILE

| Student | Dan | Date: | April 24, 1996 |

ACTIVITY	Id Time	Resources	Choice	Initiate	Skills	Interact	Problem Solve	COMMENTS
HOME (Activity within property boundaries of home or personal space)									
Alone — Throw at lights	NA	NA	NA	NA	I	NA	NA	
Whirling ride	I	NA	I	I	I	NA	NA	
Feel blowing warm air	NA	NA	NA	NA	I	NA	NA	
With Others — Listen to music with mom	PA	TA	PA	E	I	E	TA	
COMMUNITY (Activity beyond property boundaries of home)									
Alone								
With Others								
SCHOOL/WORK (Activity during recess, breaks, lunch, elective classes and extracurricular activities)									
Alone — Listen to cassette tapes	I	TA	PA	I	I	NA	TA	
Create loud noises-fire alarm	NA	NA	NA	NA	NA	NA	NA	
With Others — Record voices on cassette	E	NA	I	I	I	PA	TA	

Record enjoyed activities engaged in for at least 15 minutes, 12 times a year.
Enter the appropriate code using the following:

I	=	Independently completes without cue, or prompt.
E	=	Emerging; knows what the activity is about, or can partially complete it without adaptations.
PA	=	Participates with adaptations at predetermined level.
TA	=	Total assistance needed to complete.
NA	=	Not applicable; not required in activity, or unconventional activity in which skill is not defined.

Dan's Leisure Lifestyle Profile shows that he has several activities that he does alone at home, but only one that he does with anyone else. The activities that he does alone are non-conventional. Like most of us, the majority of Dan's free time is spent at home. He needs assistance to develop additional interests and skills for activities that he does at home by himself, as well as with others. The *Immediate Component* offers an approach to develop more conventional activities for him to do by himself at home. For instance, he might enjoy using an "Airpopper" to make popcorn, since he likes warm moving air. The *Exposure Component* may help expand his activities with others at home by providing systematic exposure to age-appropriate activities of potential interest to Dan and important people in his life.

Dan has a limited number of things that he does alone or with others at school. Due to the nature of Dan's disabilities, he is seldom alone at school. However, he still needs to be able to occupy free time by himself at times such as homeroom, break, and lunch, utilizing the *Immediate Component*. The *Exposure* and *Training Components*, through elective classes and extracurricular activities, could expand his interests and skills in other activities. For instance, he might enjoy playing a percussion instrument in the band, since he likes creating loud noises by breaking the glass on fire alarms.

Dan is not involved in community activities at this point. Since his disabilities make it difficult for him to be alone in the community, identifying community activities that his family members and friends might do with him is important.

The profile provides information for prioritizing necessary related skills for instruction. Training in all the related skills for each activity will become a focus for Dan once there are preferred activities in each grid.

Parent/Caregiver Interview

A parent/caregiver interview is important, if someone other than the parent or primary caregiver is doing the assessment. A structured interview with the parent(s) and/or others who know the individual well can gather valuable information efficiently in an hour or less. The Leisure Lifestyle Profile can be used to structure and record the information gathered in the interview.

Some key areas about which to ask questions are: activity preferences, frequency of participation, location of participation, assistance needed and shared family interests. The interviewer should use open-ended questions to gather information. The following provides some sample questions for generating information about the individual's interests and leisure pattern.

- What does your son/daughter do during unstructured time at home? school? community settings?
- What special interests does your son/daughter have?
- How does s/he express interest?
- Describe what s/he does in that activity.
- How often does s/he do that activity? For how long?
- Where does s/he do that activity?
- Who does s/he do the activity with?
- How does s/he get involved in the activity?
- What new activities would you like your son/daughter to participate in?
- What has kept your son/daughter from being involved in this activity in the past?
- Describe what your son/daughter does on a typical Saturday. Describe a typical day after school.

The information generated from these questions helps guide decision-making. Knowing what an individual actually does in an activity is important because it indicates the skill level and type of interests. For instance, if we know that a child's playing with trucks consists of spinning their wheels, we might guess that the interest is really in spinning objects. If basketball is listed as a special interest, it could mean throwing a basketball in the air and catching it, bouncing it, throwing it into a hoop, playing "Horse" with one or more peers, or playing regular basketball. Each of these represents different levels of leisure and related skills.

The frequency and length of time that an individual engages in an activity can suggest the amount of interest and opportunity. The places where an individual does activities can indicate knowledge of community and personal resources, opportunity, as well as preference for certain types of places. For instance, an individual may like to swim only in lakes because s/he does not like chlorine, crowds or being restricted. How an individual gets involved in an activity helps identify self-initiation, motivation and awareness of resources. Identifying present leisure partners helps assess present social interaction skills for activities, as well as who is presently available to do activities with the individual.

Sometimes when a parent or other caregiver is not available for a face-to-face interview, an alternative method may be necessary. A telephone interview with responses written on the Leisure Lifestyle Profile is one option. Another is to send home a questionnaire for parents or caregivers to complete and return. Appendix C provides a useful form (The Leisure Behavior Questionnaire) that can be sent home to parents or caregivers. The primary drawbacks to this approach are that not everyone will respond and that it may be difficult to clarify information.

Interview with the Individual

Information about an individual's leisure interests and skills can sometimes be gathered through an interview with the person. Since answering questions is generally difficult for even the most verbal person with autism, the interview needs to be carefully structured. It should be done by a person that the individual knows well during a time when s/he is used to answering questions. It should begin with an explanation of the purpose of the interview, what will happen and how long it will take. Pictures of activities may help to generate responses. Putting the questions in the form of a request can make the type of response you are seeking more clear to the individual. The following are some examples of request questions to ask.

> - Tell me three things that you like to do.
> - Tell me one thing that you do really well.
> - Tell me one thing that you like to do with your mother; your father; your brother; your sister; etc.
> - Tell me two things that you do at home for fun.
> - Tell me one thing that you like to do in physical education.
> - Tell me one thing that you would like to learn.

The anxiety of being "put on the spot" may make it difficult for some individuals with autism to respond to these requests. Those that write may respond better by giving written answers. The responses may be the most complete, if they are written during a time when they are used to writing new information, such as written language time at school.

Direct Observation Assessment

One of the best methods of gathering information about an individual's leisure pattern and skills is through direct observation of how free time is presently being spent. It is particularly useful when little is known about the individual's interests and skills, and is the primary method used in ongoing assessment during the *Immediate, Exposure,* and *Training Components*. The individual with autism may be observed during free time at home or in unstructured times at school, such as arrival, centers, recess, and breaks to assess what s/he does during naturally-occurring situations.

An alternative way of doing direct observation is to set up a free time with a variety of leisure materials that are age-appropriate and representative of those commonly found in school and home environments. Since it may be difficult to develop a list of age-appropriate leisure activities, the Leisure/Recreation portion of the Age-Appropriate Activity List, located in Appendix A, can be used for this purpose. The list divides the activities into categories involving media, exercise, games/crafts/hobbies, events and other.

There should be at least six items which provide opportunity for different types of use and interaction. For example, a magazine would provide an opportunity for solitary activity, whereas a ball would provide the opportunity for social interaction. The area should be arranged so that different types of activities, such as table activities and physical activities, can occur. The adult should avoid direct participation in an activity, unless involvement is requested by an individual.

The adult should explain that this is free time and that the individual can do what s/he wants in that area. After an adjustment period of at least five minutes, observations of what the individual does can be recorded. The observer records which materials are used, how the materials are used, and the length of time it was used. Materials that the individual uses are usually well-liked. The length of time spent independently in a leisure activity is particularly important to assess because of its relevance to most home situations where caregivers cannot constantly supervise the individual.

Observations of behaviors can be recorded on the Leisure Observation Sheet provided in Appendix B for four consecutive five-minute periods. The five-minute intervals can be signaled by a timer. Initially, four to six days of observation may be necessary to get adequate information. The Leisure Observation Sheet helps code the individual's social level, interaction skills and the nature of his/her involvement in the activity.

The individual's social level during each five-minute interval is noted on the Leisure Observation Sheet using the following codes:

Watches Others: exhibits no behavior other than as an on-looker; is aware of others and is observing them

No Activity: unoccupied behavior, such as staring into space or self-stimulation, such as rocking; no contact with an external object or another person

Plays Alone: plays alone with an object that is different than those used by peers within close proximity

Plays Beside Peers: approximates the action of one or more peers, but does not interact

Interacts With Peers: interacts with peers doing same or similar activity; includes borrowing or loaning equipment

Engages in Cooperative Play: mutually interacts with peers in doing an activity; activity can not continue without cooperation, e.g.. playing "catch" or "checkers."

All of the individual's social interactions during each five-minute interval is recorded on the Leisure Observation Sheet. The sheet identifies whether the individual

- interacts with adults and/or peers
- initiates and/or responds to social interactions
- interacts only briefly
- interacts in a continual or long-term manner.

The nature of the individual's involvement in the activity, such as materials used and how they were used, is also described on the Leisure Observation Sheet. This provides valuable information such as preferences, skill level, attention span, self-initiation, and social interaction. Five-minute intervals are necessary to identify activity intent. For instance, it would be easy to assume that an individual who picks up a game of "checkers," takes it to the table, opens the box, and places the board next to a peer is going to play the game cooperatively with the peer. However, during the five-minute period, the individual may ignore the peer and stack the game pieces in different ways alone.

Assessing the Leisure and Sensory Preferences of the Individual

Individuals with autism can learn to do almost any leisure activity, but if it is not a preference it is unlikely to be pursued. The development of leisure must be guided by preferences and choices that are very individual. An individual is more likely to play independently with materials that s/he prefers. Some elements in leisure activities that may be motivating for individuals with autism include the repetitive manipulation of objects, repetitive movement, visually stimulating objects, music, putting things in order, intense sensory stimulation, or fitting objects into spaces. However, interests are individual enough to require careful assessment.

Information collected during interviews and observation provides important information about the individual's interests and what they find to be naturally reinforcing. Initially, it is important to know what materials s/he shows interest in now, even if s/he does not know how to use them. For instance, we know that Dan liked to manipulate objects to make noises, likes warm things against his body, likes listening to people, and likes vestibular activities.

It is difficult to assess the interests of some individuals with autism. They may express likes and dislikes in ways that are not readily understood. Generally, interest is assumed when an individual moves towards, grabs, hugs or otherwise manipulates an object. Similarly, disinterest is assumed when an individual wanders away from leisure materials. However, the individual with autism may show interest in subtler ways, such as several sidelong glances. It is important, therefore, to consult people who are familiar with how the individual expresses interest and enjoyment, such as parents, siblings, caregivers and friends. The ongoing assessment information in the *Immediate* and *Exposure Components* will provide additional information on preferences.

Individuals with autism tend to interact more with leisure materials that provide sensory feedback, such as lights, sounds, movement and tactile sensation. One unique feature of the Components of Leisure Development is identifying and using the individual's preferences for specific types of sensory feedback.

Parents and caregivers frequently know what sensory stimulation the child seeks. Sometimes preferences are clear by what the individual normally does. For instance, Dan lies over heat registers when he is not otherwise occupied and shows excitement by flapping his hands when he is assisted with using a hair dryer. He likes warm moving air. Julie enjoyed watching flashing lights before she got interested in electronic games.

Sometimes additional assessment needs to be done to determine sensory preferences. A small number of leisure materials that provide different sensory stimuli can be presented to the individual with autism and their response can be recorded. A sample list of sensory materials can be found in Chapter 4. Observing and recording how an individual commonly uses specific leisure materials, and then determining the sensory feedback provided, is important in assessing sensory preferences.

Assessing the Leisure Preferences of Family and Friends

One of the difficulties encountered by many individuals with autism is depending on family and service providers for the opportunities to learn and engage in leisure activities. To expand leisure options, for individuals who may always need some level of support for participation, it is important to identify potential leisure partners and possible common interests with family and friends. This will expand the number of opportunities that the individual has to practice and continue to enjoy activities that s/he has learned. Two methods of gathering information about the interests of family members and friends are an open-ended questionnaire (the Leisure Interest Inventory) and a forced-choice survey (the Leisure Interest Survey).

The Leisure Interest Inventory for Friends & Family

One method of gathering information about leisure preferences of family and friends is a questionnaire with open-ended questions. The Leisure Interest Inventory for Friends & Family was developed to be used to identify potential activities that important people in the individual's life would be interested in doing with him or her. It serves as a platform for creative discussion regarding possible leisure involvement for the individual and how it could be accomplished, including identifying buddies, transportation sources, and leisure resources. A blank copy of the Leisure Interest Inventory for Friends & Family can be found in Appendix B.

An example of a filled-in copy of the Leisure Interest Inventory by Dan's friend, Bert Smith, is provided below. This inventory provides important information regarding Bert's common interests with Dan and how he might be a leisure partner for Dan. Leisure Interest Inventories completed by other friends and family members helped identify potential activities and leisure partners to further expand Dan's leisure opportunities.

LEISURE INTEREST INVENTORY
for
FRIENDS AND FAMILY

Name: *Bert Smith*   **Date:** *May 10, 1996*

Directions: The purpose of this inventory is to determine the types of activities that you enjoy doing. It will, also, be used to identify possible leisure opportunities for your friend. Please take the time to think about your own leisure and complete this inventory.

1. **List what you do for enjoyment or relaxation.**
   - When you get home from school or work: *Sleep, workout, swim, play sports, hot tub/Jacuzzi, drive, run, walk, shop, visit with friends and family, eat*
   - After dinner: *Relax, sleep, talk to friends, go to or watch a movie at home, drive, visit with family, go for a Jacuzzi*
   - During break times at school or work: *Eat*
   - During lunch: *Eat*

2. **What do you like to do for exercise or fitness?** *Lift weights, play racquet sports, swim, walk, run, hike, snow ski, boating, jet ski, sports in general, go rollerblading*

3. **List clubs or groups in which you participate:**
   - *member ski-racing team*
   - *member RiverPlace Athletic Club*
   -

4. **List classes you have taken for fun in the last two years:**
   - *shop*
   - *weight training*
   - *T.A. for special education*

5. **List some activities you enjoy doing.**
   With your family:
   - *hiking*
   - *camping*
   - *fishing*
   - *exercising*

   With your family:
   - *partying*
   - *sports*
   - *going out*

The Leisure Interest Survey

Another approach to gathering information about leisure preferences is a forced-choice survey in which the possible leisure activities are predetermined. The first step in developing a forced-choice survey for leisure is to prepare a list of age-appropriate activities that are available in the local area.

As previously mentioned, the Leisure/Recreation portion of the Age-Appropriate Activity List, located in Appendix A, provides a list of age-appropriate activities. The Age-Appropriate Activity List was developed by the Elementary/Secondary System of the University of Oregon's Specialized Training Program. Although it does not list all possibilities, it covers a wider range of activities than may be generated by an open-ended format. This list can be updated according to local availability of activities. Since it does not include the less-structured activities typical of an age group, such as "cruising" and "hanging out" for adolescents, it is important to ask what other activities might be done by same-age peers.

The Leisure Interest Survey is an example of a forced-choice survey to determine leisure interests of family members and friends. A blank Leisure Interest Survey can be found in Appendix B. The first column is blank so that a list of age-appropriate activities available in your community can be added. The questions asked during the survey are:
- Do you enjoy this activity?
- Did you do this activity in the last month? How often?
- Does anyone else in the family enjoy this activity?
- Where do you do this activity?
- Who do you do this activity with?
- Would you like to do this activity with your special friends?

Dan's family and friends completed the Leisure Interest Survey. Because of Dan's age, it utilized the 16+ portion of the Age-Appropriate Activity List. Dan's friend, Bert Smith, completed the first page of the Survey that follows.

LEISURE INTEREST SURVEY

NAME: Bert Smith　　**DATE:** May 10, 1996　　**AGE:** 17

EXERCISE/ ACTIVITY	Do you enjoy it?	Did you do it in the last month?	How often?	Does anyone else in the family do it?	Where did you do it?	Who do you do it with?	Would you like to do it with your special friend?	COMMENTS
Walking	yes	yes	daily	yes	park/sch	friends	yes	
Jogging	yes	yes	2x	yes	park/sch	friends	yes	
Riding a Bike	yes	yes		no	park/nei	myself	yes	
Playing Catch	yes	yes	10x	yes	school/pk	friends	yes	
Skill-Building Classes	so, so	yes	daily	yes	school	class-mates	yes	
Swimming	sometime	yes	10x	yes	club/river	friends	yes	
Aerobics/Slimnas-tic/Jazzercise	sometime	yes	2x	yes	club	friends	yes	
Using Equipment	yes	yes	everyday	no	club/sch	fri/class-mates	yes	I worked at the RiverPlace Athletic Club and I like working out very much.
Weight Training	yes	yes	everyday	no	club/sch	fri/class-mates	yes	
Playing Racquet Sports	yes	yes	15x	yes	club/park	friends	yes	I love to play tennis, racquetball and squash. I play sometimes in tournaments.
Skating/Rollerblde	yes	yes	2x	no	wtrfront	freinds	yes	
Skateboarding	no	no					yes	
Dance Classes	no	no					maybe	
Volleyball/Soccer	yes	yes	5x	no	park/club	friends	yes	
Being Team Mgr	no						maybe	I don't like managing because I like to play.
Golfing	yes	no	1x	no	rippl.riv.	friends	yes	
Horseback Riding	no						maybe	
Hiking/Backpack.	yes	yes	1x	yes	desch.riv.	friends	yes	
Snow Shoeing	no							
Skiing	yes	yes	8x	no	mt.hood	friends	yes	I love snow skiing. I ski on a team/ we race/ our team is sponsored by a ski shop in PDX.
Boating/Jet Skiing	yes	no	5x	yes	river	team/ friends	yes	
Ping Pong	no						maybe	

Comments: I would love to work with Dan in any of these categories

Many suggestions came from Bert's survey and the ensuing meeting with Dan's family and friends. One successful development was that Bert became Dan's work-out buddy at a private athletic club where Dan and his mother are members. The club allowed Bert to participate free as Dan's "personal trainer."

Selection of Leisure Materials and Activities

The selection of appropriate leisure materials and activities may be time-consuming. However, the systematic matching of activities and individuals ensure a more effective and meaningful program and reduces the time spent trying new activities and teaching strategies.

Community Referenced Activities

Many age-appropriate activities are listed in the Age-Appropriate Activities List in Appendix A. However, many of these may not be feasible or available in a community. Every community has different opportunities for leisure in the home, school/work, and community. Opportunities in urban areas are different than in sparsely populated rural areas. Different organizations may provide leisure opportunities in these settings. For instance, cities may have park and recreation departments, whereas rural areas may have granges or 4-H clubs. In some areas private art and music instruction might be more prevalent than extracurricular art club or band.

To make training for a leisure activity worthwhile the individual must have continued opportunities for participation in the activity after training. Activities that are already in the individual's home, school/work and/or community, along with those that can be easily purchased from nearby stores or catalogs, should be considered first.

The Natural Settings & Resources for Activities Form provides a community-referenced listing of age-appropriate activities in conjunction with where they are commonly performed or available. It was developed to identify the natural settings and resources for activities in communities for individuals of various ages. The Form is a tool to identify potential leisure activities for inclusion on individualized plans, to determine natural settings for instruction, and to identify other places for generalization of leisure skills. A blank Natural Settings & Resources for Activities Form can be found in Appendix B.

The Natural Settings & Resources for Activities Form is divided into three major environments: school, community and home. The school section includes the times where there are naturally occurring opportunities to learn or participate in leisure activities, such as break/between classes, recess, extracurricular activities, and elective classes. The community section includes the places or agencies that offer these kinds of activities. Some specific clubs and types of commercial facilities can be listed. The home section includes whether the activity is done inside the house or outside in the yard/neighborhood.

The following two sample pages from the Natural Settings & Resources for Activities Form illustrates this approach. It was specifically completed for high school students in Portland, Oregon and indicates where activities are commonly performed or available. Portland has a Parks Bureau (with parks/playgrounds, outdoor programs, community centers, and community schools), community colleges, clubs/organizations, and commercial recreation opportunities. Some specific clubs and other types of commercial facilities are listed; however, the possibilities are too extensive for this list.

The Natural Settings & Resources for Activities Form for Portland has been useful in determining places and times to train Dan and his age-peers in activities. It has, also, been helpful in identifying places to expand participation in activities that they already like.

Criteria for Selection of Leisure Materials and Activities

Once community-referenced activities have been identified, the appropriateness of potential activities needs to be assessed. When used with Components of Leisure Development, activities selected should meet the following selection criteria:
- the activity should be enjoyed by same-age peers in that community
- the activity should be readily available in the community
- the activity should be easily used in a variety of environments and situations
- the activity should be economically feasible
- the activity should have properties, such as sensory feedback, that elicit attention or are otherwise naturally reinforcing
- the activity should be of interest to family members and friends
- the activity should have the potential of being performed at least twelve times a year.

NATURAL SETTINGS & RESOURCES FOR ACTIVITIES

LEISURE ACTIVITIES Games/Crafts/Hobbies	SCHOOL Break/Between Classes	SCHOOL Recess	SCHOOL Extracurricular	SCHOOL Elective Classes/Specials	COMMUNITY Parks Bureau Parks/Playgrounds	COMMUNITY Parks Bureau Outdoor Program	COMMUNITY Parks Bureau Community Schools	COMMUNITY Parks Bureau Community Center	COMMUNITY Community Colleges	COMMUNITY Clubs/Organizations	COMMUNITY Commercial Recreation	HOME Outside	HOME Inside
Darts											Taverns		✓
Computer Games	✓	✓											✓
Hand-held Video Games	✓	✓			✓								✓
Video Games									✓		Video Arcade		✓
Card Games	✓	✓			✓		✓	✓	✓	Bridge Club			✓
Table Games	✓	✓	✓										✓
Puzzles	✓	✓											✓
Needle Crafts	✓						✓	✓		Craft Store			✓
Bowling										Leagues	Alleys		
Billiards/Pool								✓			Parlors/Taverns		✓
Instrument Playing			✓		✓		✓	✓	✓	Community Orchestra	Music Store		✓
Collections	✓									✓			✓
Kite/Model Plane Flying						✓						✓	
Art Classes/Projects			✓	✓			✓	✓	✓	✓	Art Centers		✓
Photography			✓	✓			✓	✓	✓	✓	Photo Store	✓	✓
Woodworking				✓			✓	✓	✓				✓
Gardening								✓	✓	Garden Club		✓	✓
Lawn Games												✓	

NATURAL SETTINGS & RESOURCES FOR ACTIVITIES

LEISURE ACTIVITIES	SCHOOL - Break/Between Classes	SCHOOL - Recess	SCHOOL - Extracurricular	SCHOOL - Elective Classes/Specials	COMMUNITY - Parks Bureau - Parks/Playgrounds	COMMUNITY - Parks Bureau - Outdoor Program	COMMUNITY - Parks Bureau - Community Schools	COMMUNITY - Parks Bureau - Community Center	COMMUNITY - Community Colleges	COMMUNITY - Clubs/Organizations	COMMUNITY - Commercial Recreation	HOME - Outside	HOME - Inside
Walking					✓					Volksmarche		✓	
Jogging			✓	✓	✓					Y's, Fun Run		✓	
Riding a Bike	✓				✓	✓				Wheelmen	Rental	✓	
Playing Catch		✓			✓							✓	
Attending Skill-Building Classes			✓	✓		✓	✓	✓	✓	✓	✓	✓	✓
Swimming							✓	✓	✓	Y's	Fitness Cntr	✓	✓
Participating in Aerobics/Slimnastics/Jazzercise Class				✓				✓	✓		Fitness Cntr		✓
Using Exercise Equipment				✓				✓	✓	Y's	Fitness Cntr		✓
Weight Training				✓			✓	✓	✓	Y's	Fitness Cntr		✓
Playing Racquet Sports					✓			✓	✓	Y's	Health Club	✓	
Skating					✓			✓			Rinks	✓	
Skateboarding	✓											✓	
Participating in Dance Classes				✓			✓	✓	✓	Square Dance & Other Clubs	Dance Studio		✓
Playing Volleyball/Soccer			✓	✓			✓			Leagues		✓	
Being a Team Manager			✓							Leagues		✓	
Golfing							✓		✓		Golf Course	✓	
Horseback Riding						✓				4-H	Stable	✓	
Hiking/Backpacking						✓				Sierra Club	Outfitters	✓	
Snow Shoeing						✓				Mazamas	Outfitters	✓	
Skiing						✓				Numerous	Areas	✓	
Boating							✓			Numerous	Numerous	✓	
Ping Pong								✓		Boys' Club			✓

Summary

Leisure assessment is critical to the selection of leisure materials and activities that relate to the unique needs of the individual. There are many ways that an individual's leisure competencies and interests can be assessed. Assessment methods need to be chosen based on what is already known about the individual with autism. In this chapter, a variety of approaches have been discussed with specific examples.

The systematic selection of materials and activities based upon this assessment will ensure more effective and meaningful participation during leisure, even though it may appear time consuming.

Chapter 4

The Immediate Component of Leisure Development

The inability of individuals with autism to entertain themselves appropriately and to cope with unstructured time has often been identified by parents and teachers as a major problem. Unstructured time may include waiting periods while in the community, brief periods between structured time at school or free time at home. These times may also include waiting at the doctor's office, waiting for the bus or waiting for dinner. Other potentially difficult times might include riding in the bus or car or brief times between structured activities at school. These short, unstructured times may be very difficult for the individual with autism and may be problematic for individuals with autism to occupy themselves appropriately.

The purpose of the *Immediate Component* is to provide sensory feedback and meaningful occupation to the individual with autism for short periods of leisure time. This is primarily accomplished by identifying and using toys, games and other materials. The goal of this Component is to provide the individual with autism the proper materials, based on their sensory preferences, to occupy short amounts of time.

Key Elements of the Immediate Component
The key elements of the Immediate Component are: • meaningful occupation of unstructured time • untrained activities with minimal supervision • based on sensory preferences • self determined use • age appropriate materials • ongoing assessment

Meaningful Occupation of Unstructured Time

Meaningful activities and materials are those which the individual enjoys engaging in. When considering which meaningful materials and activities should be selected for the *Immediate Component*, one must keep in mind not only the age-appropriateness of the materials, but also safety issues and the sensory qualities of the materials.

Portability is also a factor to consider in this Component. This is particularly important for community activities since parents or staff cannot always anticipate when the individual with autism may need to occupy short amounts of time. Refer to the Portable Leisure Materials List provided nearby. This list gives information on the primary sensory feature, age-appropriateness, and approximate price of some easily available materials.

There are some large motor activities that could be used to occupy short amounts of time, even though these materials are not portable. Examples of such non-portable activities may include the mini-trampoline, a Sit-n-Spin, or Hop-a-Roo Ride-on Ball.

Untrained Activities with Minimal Supervision

Because these unstructured times are short and adults are usually occupied with other matters, minimal supervision should be required for good *Immediate Component* activities. The materials available during this Component should be highly motivating so the individual will be motivated to manipulate them without direction. The reason these materials need little training and supervision is that the objects themselves dictate what to do with them. Appropriate use of these materials is not the major concern in the *Immediate Component*. However, safety should always be addressed.

Access to these materials should be given only during these unstructured times so that the individual will be motivated to interact with them and not get bored. The manner in which these materials are presented can vary. For example, a few portable materials that give the individual the sensory feedback that s/he prefers may be put in a fanny pack to take into the community to use during waiting times. At home, during free time, a basket may be presented at times when s/he should be occupied for short amounts to time. At school, materials could be given to a student at the end of a work session and before the next activity begins.

Sensory Preferences

Materials in the *Immediate Component* need to give the sensory feedback that the individual with autism prefers or even needs. If careful consideration is given to the individual's sensory preference, the material will be highly reinforcing. Methods to assess the individual's sensory preference were discussed in Chapter 3.

Individuals with autism may process sensory information differently then we do. This processing can lead to either a preference for certain sensory input or an over-sensitivity to certain sensory input. Because of this preference or sensitivity, individuals will choose materials or activities that give them the sensory feedback they prefer and they will avoid materials or activities that they are sensitive to.

Some sensory areas that an individual with autism might have preferences in or sensitivities to are the auditory, visual, and/or tactile senses. Nearby is reproduced the Portable Leisure Materials List. The following examples for Dan, Julie and John, the three individuals with autism introduced in Chapter 1, can be found on the list.

In Dan's case, to give him the auditory feedback he prefers, you might give him a simplified musical instrument such as a Microjammer guitar. He may also enjoy a cassette player with or without headphones. Julie's preference for electronic games and the visual feedback it provides can still be used. However, it is necessary to expand her choices. Other choices for Julie may include visual stimulation objects such as Pocketfuls or Orbiter II, comic books or books about video characters. For John, there are several options. For his preference to bang objects, a hammer and peg board may be appropriate. A "talking" beeper or shaver and/or "talking" books such as the Golden SeeknSound might provide the auditory input he seeks.

PORTABLE LEISURE MATERIALS LIST

PRIMARY SENSORY FEATURE	ITEM	AGE APPROPRIATE	APPROXIMATE PRICE
Tactile	Dinoball		2.99
Tactile	Koosh Ball and Critter Koosh (soft spikes)	3 and up	3.99 to 5.99
Tactile	Bongo Ball (hard spikes)	1 and up	2.99
Tactile	Fur Ball (fuzzy)	5 and up	2.99
Tactile	Gak and Gak Pak	5 and up	3.99 to 7.99
Tactile	Vector Flector	7 and up	10.50
Tactile	Glue Slug	9 and up	6.00
Tactile	Mini 4" Fun Fan	4 and up	6.99
Tactile-Visual	Crystal Putty (with sparkles)	5 and up	1.99
Tactile-Visual	Dizzy Doodler - Rainbow Writer - Pop Top Doodler	5 and up	3.99 to 8.99
Tactile-Visual	Spirograph (pocket size)	3 and up	7.99
Tactile-Visual	Transformers	7 to 12	3.99 to 19.99
Tactile-Visual	Lacing Cards	3 to 7	5.50 and up
Tactile-Visual	Magnet Sculptor	8 and up	4.95
Tactile-Visual	Roll & Stamps	2 and up	4.99
Tactile-Visual	Bumble Ball - Squiggle Ball - Bumble Buddies - Looney Ball	18 months to 5 years	5.99 to 14.99
Visual	Bubble Pen Set	5 to 11	2.99

36

PORTABLE LEISURE MATERIALS LIST cont.

PRIMARY SENSORY FEATURE	ITEM	AGE APPROPRIATE	APPROXIMATE PRICE
Visual	Waterfuls Series & Pocket Size	3 to 11	2.99 to 3.99
Visual	8 Gulping Guppies (wind-up)	3 to 8	2.49
Visual	Flip Flops (wind-up)	5 to 13	2.29
Visual	Nichelodeon Lazer Light (make your own show)	5 and up	9.99
Visual	Light Up Light Stick	5 and up	1.19
Visual	YoYo Glow Ball	5 and up	4.99
Visual	View Master	3 to 10	3.99 to 8.99
Visual	Ribbon Dancer / Sky Writer	5 and up	9.99
Visual	Hot Pocket Magna Doodle	3 and up	7.99
Visual-Auditory	Golden Seek -n- Sound	3 to 8	12.99 to 14.99
Visual-Auditory	Golden Sound Story	3 to 8	7.99 to 14.99
Visual-Auditory	Sound Scribblers (writes w/music)	3 and up	8.99
Visual-Auditory	Rock & Roll Tops (spins/lights/music)	5 and up	2.99
Visual-Auditory	Frustration Ball (puzzle ball)	5 and up	9.99

PORTABLE LEISURE MATERIALS LIST cont.

PRIMARY SENSORY FEATURE	ITEM	AGE APPROPRIATE	APPROXIMATE PRICE
Visual-Auditory	Handheld Electronic Games: Sports, Disney films, Lights Out, Space theme, Pocket Simon, Orbitor, Tiger Sticks, Lite 3, Jeopardy, Wheel of Fortune, Connect 4, Uno, Yahtzee, Brain Bash	7 and up	6.99 to 24.95
Auditory	Talking Beeper or Shaver	3 to 8	4.99
Auditory	Microjammers - piano, guitar, drums (2 sizes)	13 and up	4.99 to 7.99
Auditory	Zoink; Electronic Paddle Ball	8 and up	2.99
Auditory	Exploding Catch Game (sound when caught)	5 and up	5.99
Auditory	Candy Caller (w/candy) or Spacephone	5 to 12	2.99 to 3.99
Auditory	TV Controller & Flashlight	3 to 8	4.99
Auditory	Recorders that play back: Yak Bak, SFX, Mega Mouth Assortment, Talk Back Girl or Boy and Girl Jr or Boy Jr (beeper size)	3 and up	12.99 to 19.99

Self Determined Use

Self determined use means that the materials the individual with autism chooses may be used however they would like to use them, as long as they are safe and not destructive with them. Remember, the best choices for leisure materials and activities must be guided by preferences and choices that are very individual to the person with autism. The person with autism is more likely to play independently with materials that s/he prefers. Again, appropriate use of the materials is not the main focus in the *Immediate Component*. Basing the choice of materials on the individual's sensory preference will ensure that there will be self determined use of the materials and there will be little need for supervision.

Age Appropriate Materials

Consideration should be given to how age appropriate the materials are, especially those used in the community. Note that the sample materials listed for Dan, Julie and John under sensory preferences are also age appropriate.

How age appropriate a material is can often be determined by the age ranges found on the material's box or package. The Portable Leisure Materials List marks appropriate age ranges for many materials. You may also observe same age peers for ideas of what materials they interact with. When expanding choices within the *Immediate Component*, consideration should always be given to the age appropriateness of the materials.

Ongoing Assessment

Assessment of the individual's leisure skills needs to be an ongoing process and serve as the basis for changes or expansion in the *Immediate Component*. The Leisure Lifestyle Profile presented in Chapter 3 provides a form to record progress and note needed modifications. Assessment should utilize ongoing observation to determine sensory preferences or sensitivities, possible boredom and activity preferences. This information also can help in the decision making process in both the Exposure and Training Components. As in Julie's case, her tactile defensiveness should be considered when choosing activities to expose her to. For Dan, materials that give him auditory feedback should be considered. John may need large motor activities to give him the input he prefers.

Summary

The *Immediate Component* is very important to the individual with autism's development of leisure skills for short periods of unstructured time. The *Immediate Component* uses meaningful activities to fill short amounts of leisure time at home, school/work or in the community. Activities and materials for the *Immediate Component* should be meaningful to the individual, require minimal supervision, address the sensory preferences of the individual, be self-determined in their use, and be age-appropriate. The *Immediate Component* is ongoing, even while *Exposure* and *Training* is taking place, and requires ongoing assessment.

Chapter 5

The Exposure Component of Leisure Development

No one's life can be truly fulfilled without the ability to grow, broaden or expand in all areas of life. Leisure is no exception. An individual with autism needs extra assistance to explore the world of leisure opportunities. One vital component to the development of leisure skills is the systematic and structured exposure to new activities of potential interest. For the individual with autism to explore new experiences and potentially build them into interests for available leisure time can be overwhelming. This chapter describes how to apply a systematic structure, utilizing assessment and interests, to explore new materials or activities.

Key Elements of the Exposure Component
The key elements of the Exposure Component are: • a systematic, structured approach to exploration of activities • minimal training with multiple exposure • the preferences of individual, family & friends • trainer-directed exposure • age- and sensory-appropriate materials & activities • ongoing assessment.

A Systematic, Structured Approach

Individuals with autism generally have a very narrow range of interests and leisure experiences. Many times they are not exposed to a wide range of possibilities due to their lack of motivation to even participate in activities, which in turn, often occurs because they do not understand the value of the activities. Many lack the curiosity to explore and join family members or friends to experience leisure options. Some individuals with autism have difficulty understanding the meaning and purpose of new situations or they become confused from sensory overload. Social expectations that are critical in many leisure activities are often not readily clear to the individual with autism.

A systematic, structured approach means providing the individual with information such as what to expect will happen, what the whole project or activity is from start to finish, what parts are critical, and preparing for any sensory problems. A systematic, structured approach is needed to guide an individual through the exploration stage of new activities. This structure is illustrated in the accompanying Activity Cards provided in Appendix C, which offer the necessary information to the adult supervising the activity as well as for the individual with autism. The structure outlined by the Activity Cards provides the individual with autism with carefully chosen leisure experiences as well as clarifies the facilitator's role to offer understandable and comfortable exploration.

Minimal Training with Multiple Exposure

In exploring new activities, there are many uncomfortable areas for all of us. For individuals with autism new activities can be not only extremely uncomfortable, but they may not respond or they may respond in unusual ways. Minimal training, therefore, is necessary, even at the exploration level. Careful decision-making and preplanning by the facilitator, through systematic structure, can minimize the discomfort for the individual with autism. Some of the areas to explore include predetermining sensory concerns, the level of assistance or participation needed by an individual and an understanding of the activity. The exploration of a new or relatively new experience should not require a high level of skill development; the next Component, *Training*, focuses on leisure and leisure-related skill development. However, there is still a level of minimal training required in the exploration stage to ensure the accurate perception of the individual with autism.

Many individuals with autism are one-trial learners, which means they record their first experience as the way it will be every single time. Therefore, a negative or confusing experience needs to be minimized for true exploration of interest. Pre-planning and pre-teaching in a systematic structure will ensure minimal misperception during exposure. Multiple exposure or repeating experiences provides a level of comfort and understanding and may be needed to determine a true interest in an activity due to a particular day, mood, or unexpected interruption. Providing a systematic structure with minimal training of the activity can offer the opportunity to more accurately explore the long-range potential of a leisure option.

The Preferences of Individual, Family & Friends

Careful consideration must be given to the activities explored for an individual with autism. In Chapter 3, a variety of information gathering tools were discussed to determine what types of activities the individual may enjoy and participate in with family, friends or individually. There are many issues in determining which new activities could be explored. However, one of the priorities is understanding the preferences of not only the individual but the family and friends. What activities are interesting to the individual and family may offer clues as to other activities for exploration.

Trainer-Directed Exposure

Individuals with autism may not creatively explore new materials or activities on their own. They may primarily perceive new experiences through their sensory system and become repetitive in the use of materials or experiences. For example, John, who loves the movement, sound and wind of the zoo train, thinks the zoo is only for the train ride. Although he loves animals, he will not venture past the zoo train to view another part of the zoo.

Utilizing pre-planning and pre-teaching, as provided by a trainer, can ensure that exposure to new and different experiences is as broad and positive as possible. Trainer-directed structure can be a way to minimize discomfort or prevent mislearning a new activity. Positive exploration of new experiences not only builds an individual's confidence to explore it, but provides a more clear decision about whether this activity should be pursued as a viable leisure option.

Age Appropriate Materials and Activities

Age appropriate materials and activities are important in the *Exposure Component*. To assist the reader, the Leisure/Recreation portion of the Age Appropriate Activity List from the Elementary/Secondary System, Specialized Training Program, University of Oregon is presented in Appendix A. The Elementary/Secondary System divides the activities into the categories of exercise, games/crafts/hobbies, events, media and other. It does not list all the possibilities, but provides a solid start.

Consideration must be given in the planning or pre-planning stage to determine age appropriate materials as well as age appropriate use of materials. Sensory preferences must also be considered before presenting new materials. When an individual explores a new or novel material, they may first engage their sensory action, such as throwing, banging or flapping it. Pre-teaching the use of materials, rather than free exploration, may be necessary for some individuals with autism to use materials appropriately. This means the facilitator would direct and control an individual's exploration of new toys, minimizing mislearning the use of age-appropriate materials. Preferred sensory feedback can be part of age-appropriate opportunities. Examples of this include Dan's exposure to the gym for weight training, Julie exploring in Nintendo tournaments or John, who loves outdoors and walking, participating in a Volksmarch.

Ongoing Assessment

Ongoing assessment is vital in determining which activities should be repeated for multiple exposure, as well as which should be pursued during the *Training Component*. Determining which activities should be dropped or which activities could be used in the *Training Component* requires careful consideration by the individual, family and facilitator. Typically a formal data collection system is the most helpful. A way to gather simple information is provided with the Activity Cards and explained later in this chapter. You will note that the information is very basic but invaluable for the decision-making process. The format of the data form is also designed to allow some individuals to comment and chart their own interests and successes. Any incidental information or observations should be considered as well, since any pieces one can fit into the puzzle are helpful.

The Activity Cards

One way of providing a systematic, structured approach to activity exploration is to use Activity Cards. A full selection of Activity Cards are provided in Appendix C. Each Activity Card section provides information important to the development of understanding new experiences or new materials. The cards are intended to be easily understood and read by a variety of care-givers, including friends, church workers, baby-sitters, and teachers. When working with individuals with autism, a variety of strategies can assist in the learning process. Therefore, a variety of strategies are provided in the Activity Cards:
- pictorial information, in the form of line drawings
- written story information, which provides visual information and offers correct sequencing or organization
- variations in the activity, with choices to encourage expansion

Community and Social Activities have additional cards for other stages of the activity:
- "Get Ready" cards help prepare for the activity
- "The Real Thing" cards show the real experience of the activity
- "Review" cards help the individual review the activity.

The Activity Cards are only a start. A wide variety of activities are possible to explore. Be creative; but apply pre-planning and a highly structured approach, as outlined in these Cards. Remember, exploring activities for individuals may need to be systematic and structured, but they should be fun, too!

Refer to the the sample Activity Card. The numbers correspond to the following numbered sections, which provide a detailed description of the Activity Card use and organization.

1) **The first picture** illustrates scheduling, materials or introductory visual images of the activity.
2) **The written title** of the activity is provided at the top of the card. Community/Social activities also have the subtitle ("Get Ready," "The Real Thing," or "Review") printed at the top of the card.
3) **The reason why** the activity is performed is provided. Many individuals with autism have difficulty understanding the purpose of new experiences. This is a basic reminder for the facilitator of the purpose of the activity.
4) **"Materials"** lists what materials are used in the activity. Organization and pre-planning are crucial. This lists what is needed to prepare for the activity and the materials which need to be collected and made ready to explore.
5) **"General Rule of Thumb"** provides the basic breakdown of steps in completing an activity. Due to limited space, each step may be stated in very general terms. This is where the facilitator's knowledge of the individual with autism is critical, to know exactly how much the steps need to be further simplified.

Sections 6 - 9 may include additional information to further expand or prepare for the activity:

6) **"Choices"** lists the options provided by an activity. Choices allows for more independence and nurtures self-esteem. This information can be presented on any level the individual needs.
7) **"Do It Yourself"** encourages independence. Independence can be accomplishing a task all by yourself or, for some, knowing how and when to ask for help. Ideas presented here assume the individual is working on the ability to perform a task without much assistance. However, it provides alternative ways to feel independent and successful.
8) **"Furthermore"** consists of suggestions for modifying parts of the activity. Use of the modification is guided by the facilitators decision-making process. In some cases, this may mean breaking down or expanding the activity.
9) **"Cautions"** may be found on some of the Activity Cards. This section provides reminders that individuals with autism may have potentially dangerous behaviors, such as biting or chewing electrical cords, throwing heavy objects, and other reactions not buffered with a sense of danger. The caution reminders pertain to possible trouble areas within the activity.

10) **Activity Stories** are provided on the back of each card. These provide the activity's sequence in written form. For some individuals with autism the pre-planning or pre-teaching process includes thinking through what is to happen. In this way it is clear what expectations are, what will be happening and what the end result will look like. More than the specific steps to success, these activity stories attempt to assist the individual by offering information on what will be expected of them and what they can expect of the new or less-familiar experience. The Social Story approach developed by Carol Gray could further enhance the individual's understanding of the activity.

11) **Visual Presentation.** These sketches provide visual information for the sequence of the activity or choice within the activity. The same sketch is not repeated in a sequence. Some cutting and pasting of these activities may be necessary. Some visual presentations will offer futher explanations by caption.

As stated previously, the cards are written and organized in a style that is easily understood by a variety of care givers. They were first used by high school students working in a summer program as a means of structuring the exploration of the community, but also to structure arts and craft time. Most of the cards are structured to encourage exploration of new activities. However, the section labeled "Other" offers some simple activities for use by babysitters or other respite care providers.

The Activity Cards

THE ZOO (The Real Thing)

Why Are We Doing This?
FUN!! Exposure to real life animals.

Materials:
Money for admission and/or snack
Prepared picnic lunch

General Rule Of Thumb:
1. Do preparation activity first.
2. Get there safely. Practice and review rules for the zoo. (i.e. stay with buddy, etc.)
3. Allow the child, within reason, to set the amount of time to view each animal.
4. There are plenty of opportunities to practice language skills. "What do you see?" "What are they doing?"
5. Take a break. Practice ordering a snack or eat the lunch you have prepared (see lunch preparation).
6. Be sure to give the child adequate warning for when it will be time to go. "We will see the penguins and then we will leave."

Choices:
As mentioned, allow the child to determine how long to stay at each animal. If you order a snack or drink let the child choose what he/she wants.

Do It Yourself:
Encourage the child to ask questions.

And Furthermore:
Practice language skills such as labeling. You might want to bring along the pictures or objects you used in the preparation activity to relate to what they are seeing in person.

Cautions:
Keep a good eye on your child. Make sure they are close by. Also check to see if the crowd is "getting to him" or is she bored looking at the sleeping lion?

Activity Story

Today I am going to the zoo.

I will see many animals. There may be many people there too.

Sometimes the animals or the people make noises. I will be okay because I will walk away if the noise is loud.

Sometimes the animals smell different. I may think they smell bad. It's okay because I can walk away from those animals.

When I walk away or walk around the zoo I will walk with a friend or my family.

If I am hungry or need the bathroom I will tell my friend or family. I know where to go because I think about my map. My map tells where places are at the zoo.

If I get tired I can tell my friend or family. We can sit and rest.

After we have seen the animals we will go back to the car. It will be time to go home (back to school).

Visual Presentation

1. Going to the zoo 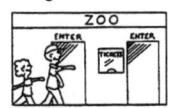
2. Looking at the animals from the map 
3. I can ask to go to the bathroom 
4. Eating at the zoo 
5. Zoo 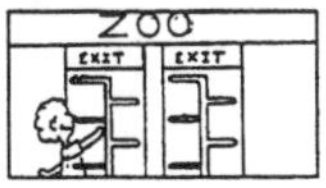
6. Exit

Activity Assessment Card

Reviewing the experiences of individuals with autism is a critical part of understanding which new activity should move on to the *Training Component*. By using a systematic, structured approach, valuable information in a variety of areas can be learned about each individual. However, in general, there are four areas we are most interested in. The following is a description of the sample Activity Assessment Card. A blank Assessment Card designed to accompany the Activity Cards is found in Appendix C.

1) **Level of Interest.** Was the activity interesting? not interesting? or just so-so?
2) **Participation.** How willing or how skilled was the individual in engaging in the activity? What kind of assistance was needed? The family or teacher will know if the level is typical and whether it reflects enthusiasm or resistance.
3) **Communication.** A critical goal for individuals with autism is communication. New or novel experiences sometimes bring out more or less communication. How did the individual communicate and how was it interpreted? Again, a parent or teacher may interpret the communication described as typical or not.
4) **Materials.** A record of how the materials were used can be helpful. In some activities, recording how the individual explored the new activity is the critical focus. For other experiences, it can lend insight into the sensory or activity preferences of individuals with autism.

Further information may be helpful for families. The type of collection may be easily expanded as the family requests. The visuals provided in each category are available for two purposes. First, it is a quick, easy assessment by a caregiver, such as a baby-sitter, who does not have a great deal of time for recording. Secondly, some individuals with autism may independently score their own feelings toward the activity through the use of a series of facial symbols. Any other collection method can be used, as long as it provides information as to how the new activity was experienced and whether it could be tried again with or without modification.

After involvement in the *Immediate* and *Exposure Components*, Dan is involved in more activities. We knew from the Leisure Lifestyle Profile that he is doing a variety of activities, and as we asked about his participation in them, we discovered that he might not like all the activities that others structured for him. Since Dan liked throwing objects at lights, he was exposed to bowling and basketball. Despite exposure to bowling on a regular basis, Dan did not enjoy it. Although he would have a continued opportunity through a bowling league at work, bowling would not be one of his activities for *Training*. On the other hand, he enjoys "Hoop" basketball and can play the game in a variety of settings.

Activity Assessment Card

Name_____
Activity_____
Date_____

1. Level of Interest:

Pleasurable   Negative   Ho-Hum

2. Participation:

All Myself   Needed Help   No

Total Physical Assist:_____
Physical and Verbal:_____
Verbal Only:_____

3. Communication:

Great Day   Not So Good   Usual Day

Choices:_____
_____

Do It Yourself_____
_____

Comments:_____
_____

Summary

It can be very overwhelming for the individual with autism to explore new experiences and potentially build them into interests for available leisure time. The *Exposure Component* describes how to apply a systematic, structured approach, utilizing assessment and known interests, to explore new materials or activities.

The key elements of the *Exposure Component* are: 1) a systematic, structured approach to exploration of activities, 2) minimal training with multiple exposure, 3) the preferences of individual, family & friends, 4) trainer-directed exposure, 5) age and sensory appropriate materials and activities, and 6) ongoing assessment.

One way of providing a systematic, structured approach to activity exploration is to use the Activity Cards, which provide pictorial information in the form of line drawings, written story information, which provide visual information and offers correct sequencing or organization, and presents variations in the activity, with choices to encourage expansion.

Reviewing the experiences of individuals with autism is a critical part of understanding which new activity needs to move on to the *Training Component*. By using a systematic, structured approach, valuable information in a variety of areas can be learned about each individual's response to the activity. However, in general, there are four areas of greatest concern: the level of interest, the level of participation, communication responses and how materials are used.

Chapter 6

The Training Component of Leisure Development

The previous two chapters addressed untrained activities that provide sensory feedback and exposure to new materials and activities with minimal training. From these *Immediate* and *Exposure Components*, the individual's interests and skills are known and can be developed further. This chapter describes the third Component of leisure development for individuals with autism, *Training*.

The purpose of training for leisure is to develop the necessary activity and related skills for the individual to participate, as independently as possible, in enjoyed activities alone or with friends and family. As a result of the *Training Component*, individuals with autism should have a leisure lifestyle with skills and knowledge which they will enjoy and chose to use after instruction.

Key Elements of the Training Component
The key elements of the *Training Component* are: • leisure activity and related skill development • ongoing training • preferences of individual, family and friends • individualized program • community referencing • ongoing assessment.

Leisure Activity and Related Skills Development

Generally, people learn recreation activities either from friends and family members, through classes, clubs and organizations, or by reading instructions. Learning may occur through informal means, such as imitating another person swinging, or by formal instruction, such as taking a class in weaving. Individuals with autism seldom learn related skills through the informal means utilized by others. Without extra assistance in formal instruction, they are unlikely to understand or learn all the skills necessary for participation in an activity.

The motor or cognitive skills necessary to successfully participate in a specific leisure activity are called leisure activity skills. Often the activity skills for participation have been the sole focus in preparing people with autism for leisure. Many of these programs, such as Wehman and Schleien's *Leisure Programs for Handicapped Learners* and Wuerch and Voeltz's *Longitudinal Leisure Skills for Severely Handicapped Learners* have task-analyzed leisure activities to identify steps for training. These two works also address possible adaptations and instructional strategies.

Additional consideration needs to be given for individuals with autism. Most will need specific types of modifications to support their unique learning style. These modifications will be discussed in this chapter.

Although leisure activity skills are important, independent participation requires more than the skills to perform the activity itself. It also requires an awareness of free time, the identification of resources, choice-making, initiation, social interaction, and problem-solving skills related to the activity.

Activities, such as going out to recess, are often not a focus of instruction, because they appear to be fairly straight-forward. However, John, like many young children with autism, has difficulty on the playground. Although he enjoys and knows how to swing, he still needs to learn when it is time to go out to swing, whether a coat is appropriate, how to move with the class to the playground, how to wait his turn if the swings are occupied, and how to know when it is time to stop swinging. If training for participation on the playground or in other activities does not include the related skills, the individual with autism will be unable to pursue these activities as independently as possible. When an individual with autism lacks the related skills for an activity, s/he may engage in undesired or unusual behavior instead.

Many leisure training programs isolate related skills, such as choice-making or identification of free time, and teach them as separate categories. Weaknesses in incidental learning and generalization make it vital to teach the relevance of related skills specific to each activity. Therefore, the *Training Component* emphasizes the simultaneous development of specific activity and related skills.

The following information outlines the importance of the related skill areas in leisure training and suggests some basic educational supports for each area.

Awareness of Leisure and Free Time

Individuals with autism generally do not differentiate between play and work. The concept of leisure or free time as an opportunity to have fun and engage in enjoyable activities needs to be taught. Developing a concrete awareness of free time, so that the individual knows when there are opportunities to participate in leisure pursuits, is an important aspect of training. The individual needs to know the cues for times such as recess at school, break at work, or discretionary time at home, as well as what activities are appropriate at these times. Some people may learn a set of appropriate activities for these times, while others may need a written or pictorial list of possibilities for unstructured times. Some individuals with autism may continue to need a cue card of what signals free time or may need to rely on a written or pictorial schedule.

For instance, John could use a pictorial schedule with a line drawing of the playground after "centers." If it is unclear when "centers" ends, he might additionally have a series of three pictures to indicate: 1- a flashing overhead light to signal recess, 2- lining up, and 3- swinging on the playground.

Identification of Community and Personal Resources

To independently pursue an activity, it is necessary to know where it is appropriate to do it, how much money is needed, what form of transportation is available, who can participate in the activity, what equipment is needed and what to wear. Some individuals with autism may need diagrams or other visual prompts to help them remember all the materials needed for a particular activity. For instance, Julie may need a written check list for skating that she is taught to use, such as the one below.

SKATING CHECKLIST

Time & Place:	4:00 - 6:00 Tuesday Skate World 1220 NE Kelly Ave.
Money to Bring:	$1.25 to skate $1.00 for snacks $2.25
Way to Get There:	Mom will drive from school at 3:30
Friends for Skating:	Tiffany from school and sister, Bonnie
Things to Bring:	_____ skate bag _____ skates _____ socks _____ knee pads

Note that this is a checklist for personal resources only. Julie may need other written or pictorial information for skating.

Choice-Making

Individuals with autism may not understand the concept of making choices. One goal of leisure training is to enable the individual to choose what to do with free time. Choice is central to the leisure experience, because what is enjoyable to one person may be disliked by another. Having a means of making a choice that is meaningful to the individual is important.

There must be at least two different activities for there to be a choice. For an activity to be a choice, the individual should have at least the basic activity skills for participation. In some cases, the individual may only be able to choose from two options initially. Over time, the number of options for choice-making should increase.

Individuals with autism often need to be taught to choose activities during free time. Choices may be made in a variety of ways. Some individuals may need the real object in front of them, while others may choose from a written or pictorial list. For instance, Julie needs to be reminded that there are other things that she can do besides electronic games. In her purse, she could keep a laminated list of activities that she has enjoyed during the *Exposure Component* or has learned in the *Training Component*. Later she may be able to select leisure activities for an entire weekend. John, on the other hand, may pair a picture in a "choice book" with an activity. The Activity Cards in Appendix C provide additional ways that choice-making can be encouraged and taught.

Self-Initiation of Activities

The independent pursuit of leisure requires self-initiation of activities. However, individuals with autism often have difficulty initiating an activity. The other related skills of awareness of free time, identification of resources, choice-making and social interaction skills are all critical to being able to self-initiate. For some individuals, the presence of the leisure materials may initially be the best cue to begin the activity. Written or pictorial information on how to prepare and begin an activity may be needed to assist the individual with autism to initiate the activity. The activity story approach introduced in the Activity Card section of the *Exposure Component* is one example of a strategy to provide this information.

Social Interaction Skills

The nature of autism causes social interaction to be a weak area. Individuals with autism usually have difficulty identifying both when and how to interact.

Fortunately, not all leisure activities require social interaction. For instance, electronic games such as Nintendo can often be played alone. However, many leisure activities are of a cooperative or competitive nature and require social interaction with at least one other person. For instance, most card games require turn-taking, asking to join in the activity, requesting a card or cards, and other interactive behavior skills. It is often falsely assumed that the individual with autism will automatically learn these skills by simply being integrated with typical peers.

Observing the social interactions of same-age peers engaging in the activity is an excellent method to determine what social skills the individual with autism will need to be taught to participate. Training related to social skills should initially emphasize those skills needed in a shared activity or game as opposed to the more complex conversational social interactions, such as "small talk."

Basic social interaction skill, such as turn-taking, may be difficult for the individual with autism to learn without additional support. Some may learn to talk about turn-taking or other social skills without understanding the concepts. John does not understand waiting his turn when other students are using the swing, so he hits them. Although this may not be unusual developmentally, he is unlikely to wait his turn through verbal corrections and explanations.

The rule for the playground is to count to 100 and then say it is your turn. Since John can not count to 100, he could be taught to turn over a series of cards numbered 1 to 100 on a ring. He could also be taught to hold out the last card, a picture of swinging with "My Turn" written on it, to request his turn.

John also needs a concrete way to know when it is his turn in a table game, so that he does not grab materials. He could learn to receive a part of the game from the person before him when it is his turn and then pass the part on to the next person.

A possible goal for Julie is to share and take her turn with her electronic game. To make this concrete, she could be taught to hand the game to her friend when the screen reads "Player 2."

Relationships may develop based on shared interests. Activities of shared interest can be used to set a topic for a conversation. For instance, Julie might be taught to use a picture or cue card of Skate World to initiate talking with Bonnie and Tiffany on the way to skating. The cue card could include some conversation starters such as, "How do you like Skate World?" In addition, she may need a written or drawn conversational script to help her to continue the conversation.

Problem-Solving Skills

Individuals with autism often have difficulty generating alternative ways to do things. They often persist with the same solution to a problem even when it does not help. It is, therefore, often helpful to develop a variety of approaches at the beginning of training, so that the individual does not get "stuck" in one mode.

Many individuals with autism need to learn to identify a problem and ask for help, as well as to try to do something a different way. Developing and rehearsing contingency plans can prevent anxiety and frustration. Written or pictorial reminders of these contingency plans facilitate smoother participation. An example of a general problem-solving plan for Julie's art class follows:

Problem	What to Do	What to Say
Difficulty doing activity	1. Keep trying 2. Approach helper	"I need help please."
No directions/ materials	1. Approach helper 2. Do what others are doing	"I need help please." "Is this what I should do?"
Not enough materials	1. Borrow from friends or helpers	"Could I use that please?"
Seat taken	1. Find different area	"Can I share this area?"

Ongoing Training

Instruction in activity and related leisure skills must be ongoing and individualized for the individual using a systematic, structured approach. It is assumed that staff implementing the *Training Component* have a basic knowledge of behavioral and learning characteristics of individuals with autism, as well as an understanding of educational best practices. Pre-planning and preparing the instruction, as well as the individual, will ensure success. The following basic guidelines are included as a review of some areas that are of particular importance for individuals with autism.

Related Skills Integrated into Instruction

Related skills, such as identification of free time, choice-making, identification of resources, problem-solving, and social interaction should be integrated into activity instruction, so that the child will understand where and how these skills fit into the activity.

Restricted Access to Materials

Individuals with autism are often one-trial learners. They tend to continue to use materials in the same way that they initially use them whether it is appropriate or not. Since appropriate use of materials is important, access to materials required for an activity needs to be restricted to training sessions until the individual uses the materials appropriately on his or her own.

Structured Interactions with Typical Peers

Individuals with autism may not learn to interact well when their peers are also disabled. Instruction in inclusive settings can facilitate the acquisition of social skills. However, even in integrated settings, social skills need to be systematically taught.

Reinforcement

A careful assessment of what is reinforcing to the individual with autism needs to be made. Individuals with autism are not necessarily reinforced by edibles or social praise. Identifying activities or properties within the activity that are of individual interest is vital. Some individuals with autism are reinforced by completing an activity. Following the training session with a highly preferred activity will increase the probability that the first activity will be positive.

Preparation for Change

Individuals with autism have difficulty with change or things that are new. They need assistance to prepare for and adjust to change. Prepare them ahead for change and new activities with information in a visual format. Excellent examples of how to prepare an individual with autism for change or a new activity is provided in the Activity Cards in Appendix C.

A person with autism often copes better when the duration of an activity is made clear. For instance, Julie would have been very anxious if the times for skating were not included on her checklist. Time can also be indicated by timers, a sequence of line drawings, or blocks that are removed or added to a grid as time passes.

Highlighting Meaning

Individuals with autism may have difficulty understanding the relevance of events and knowing when, where, how and how long to do activities. They are usually very concrete and visual. Therefore, providing this information in a visual form is most effective. Provide clear direction, rules and routines in a manner the particular individual will understand. The Activity Direction Sheet printed nearby provides an example of the type of extra information that may be needed for an individual with autism who reads, but has difficulty following auditory directions and demonstrations well. It is for an elective class in art.

Depending upon the level of understanding of the individual, meaning may be highlighted by a real object, photographs, line drawings or written information. Examples of picture sequences and written explanations is provided in the Activity Cards (Appendix C). An example of a checklist is provided earlier in this chapter. A series of pictures or a written list of steps can continue to help the individual to do the activity more independently after instruction. An example for Julie to participate in art class follows.

ART ACTIVITY: Silk screen painting birthday cards

AMOUNT: 5 birthday cards

NEEDED MATERIALS: 5 sheets of paper, screen with frame, roller, ink, drying rack.

DIRECTIONS:

1. Get materials from silk screen shelf.

    Choose color of paper
    Choose different color of ink
    Choose screen pattern with frame

2. Put materials on your work area.

    Paper Ink & roller Screen & frame Rack

3. Insert paper in frame after teacher demonstration.

4. Roll roller in ink and then over screen from left to right.

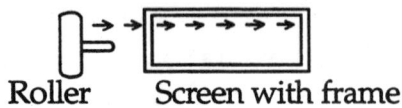

    Roller Screen with frame

5. Remove paper from screen & put on drying rack.

6. Repeat #3 - #5 until you have 5 cards.

7. Wash roller, screen & your hands.

8. Put materials back on silk screen shelf.

9. Get ready for next class. You can talk with friends now.

Clarifying Natural Cues

Individuals with autism often become prompt-dependent and wait for directions from the instructor. To develop more independence, highlight natural cues or provide visual sequences to when, where and how to do activities. When prompting is necessary, carefully fade using time-delay procedures. Instruct at the natural time for leisure, so that natural cues for participation can be learned. For Dan, the natural times at school for leisure are during break, between bells, lunch, elective classes or extracurricular activities. At work, it may be during break and lunch. For John, the times at school would include recess and play times.

Generalization

Individuals with autism may have difficulty with generalization. Instruction should be in settings where the activity is expected to occur. If it can be done in more than one setting, exposing the individual with autism to the different variables in these settings is important. For instance, Julie is likely to eventually go skating in other places than Skate World. At these other places, she may need to pay a different amount, as well as go to different areas to pay, pick up her skates and get a snack. Training in several skating places should help her generalize skills. This approach is called "general case programming."

Coping with Stress

Many individuals with autism have sensory sensitivities. Normal levels of auditory or visual input may be perceived as too much or too little. They may become overstimulated by normal stimuli. An unstructured, noisy environment often elicits undesirable behavior.

Teaching coping strategies, such as relaxation techniques, taking a break, desensitization through guided imagery procedures or Social Stories can help. Sometimes adaptations to decrease the input may also be necessary, such as visors for bright lights or personal music players, such as a Walkman, for high noise levels. In some cases, the environment can be modified, such as changing from fluorescent to incandescent bulbs or removing visual clutter. Despite coping strategies, some individuals will only be capable of participation during times of least stimulation.

Whenever the individual can tolerate it, instruct under the same conditions, such as noise and light crowding, as the individual with experience with continued participation. Sometimes the individual will need to start with less stimulating conditions and slowly increase to normal stimulation levels.

An increase in unusual or difficult behaviors probably indicates an increase in stress. Stress may only be alleviated if the individual leaves the stressful event or situation. There should always be an identified safe place to go to and a re-entry protocol.

Adaptations

Individuals with autism may need to do some leisure activity and related skills in a different way than their peers. For instance, Julie has balance problems so the wheels of her skates are tightened to give her more control. She also needs a template that she can match for the $1.25 to pay for skating.

Careful consideration needs to be given to adaptations, because they increase dependency and will need to be maintained by parents, other caregivers or professionals. For instance, Julie's template for paying for skating needs to be replaced if lost or if the price of skating changes. If the adaptations are dependent on professionals, they may fail when the professional is no longer available. Alternative ways of accomplishing a task need to be acceptable to the individual with autism, people who care about him or her as well as community members. It is desirable to have adaptations that the person with autism may be trained to eventually maintain.

Assessing needed adaptations can be done in a three-step process. First, observe same-age peers doing the activity to identify the leisure activity and related skills necessary to independently participate in the activity. Next, identify how the individual with autism presently does the activity compared to typical peers. Finally, determine what leisure activity or related skills will require instruction and/or adaptations. This approach is called an "ecological inventory" or a "discrepancy analysis."

Note the Discrepancy Analysis with Adaptation Hypothesis form for Dan that follows. This form is for swimming and illustrates the adaptations Dan will need. A blank Discrepancy Analysis form can be found in Appendix D. Using this form provides a systematic approach for studying environments and overcoming barriers to leisure development.

Preferences of Individuals, Family and Friends

Instruction must focus on activities that are known to be desired by the individual and the family, so that it will be naturally reinforcing and will be likely to motivate continued participation after training.

One of the difficulties encountered by many individuals with autism is the need to depend on family or service providers for the opportunities to learn and engage in leisure activities. Some individuals may always need some level of support for participation. For instance, although Dan is a good swimmer, he needs support to get to and participate at the Multnomah Athletic Club. He also needs support in other community leisure activities.

DISCREPANCY ANALYSIS WITH ADAPTATION HYPOTHESES

Student:	Dan	Age:	18	Date:	May 8, 1997

Activity:	Swimming	Environment:	Multnomah Athletic Club

Subenvironments:	Swimming Pool

Area	Skill	Competence	Adaptation
ID TIME	Determine appropriate times to swim	Does not read club's schedule for swim times	Personal schedule of large, bold line drawings
RESOURCES	Arrange for transportation	Inconsistently ask for ride from buddy	Taped request reminder in schedule
	Pay for membership	Does not contribute	Partial payment from earnings
CHOICE	Indicate desire to go swimming	Does not indicate	Choice board of large bold line drawings
INITIATE	3:30 p.m.: Collect swimsuit towel athletic bag membership card athletic bag snack money	Difficulty locating & collecting materials	Pre-packed bag with material always in compartments
SKILLS	Enter front door and go to locker	Difficulty locating door	Sighted guide/buddy
	Undress and put clothes in locker		
	Swim		
	Follow pool rules		
	Dress in locker room		
	Leave locker club when swimming over	Difficulty exiting	Sighted guide/buddy
INTERACT	Greet and show card at counter to staff	Greets. Trouble locating card	Card on cord around neck
	Conversation with friends	Repeats phrases	Teach conversational routines with practice tapes
	Request friend to stop at snack bar	Goes by himself	Practice tapes and reminder card
PROB SOLVE	Ask for help if forget or lose something	Does not ask for assistance	"Help" reminder card in wallet

Because friendships are often built on familiarity and shared mutual interests, the *Training Component* uses the Support Circle concept first developed by Judith Snow and Marsha Forest. A series of meetings were held with Dan's family and friends to identify who could support Dan in his leisure pursuits. Dan was encouraged to be part of these meetings. Initially all his important people being in the same room was overwhelming and Dan needed to leave the room frequently. As he grew more accustomed to the meetings, he was able to participate more.

Identifying other available activities in the community and activities of interest to Dan and his friends is vital to generating more opportunities for him. Potential leisure partners and possible common interests were identified through the forms introduced in Chapter 3: Assessment.

Bert became Dan's friend, in part because they both enjoyed woodworking at school. This approach lead to Bert being Dan's work out buddy at an athletic club.

Individualized Program

The ultimate goal of leisure training is that the individual has the related leisure skills to actively choose and engage in a variety of activities in a variety of environments. Although individuals with autism have many common difficulties and characteristics related to leisure participation, it is important to establish specific individualized objectives and identify appropriate training strategies.

The Leisure Lifestyle Profile that was introduced in Chapter 3 gives an overall picture of the balance of activities in different settings. It provides necessary information on the nature of the individual's leisure skills and pattern for planning individualized leisure training. The ongoing assessment from the *Immediate* and *Exposure Components* will provide valuable information about the individual's interests, as well as the degree of support needed to participate.

Given the ongoing information on Dan, Julie and John, some possible training activities could be selected. For instance, Dan's interest in striking things to make noise and listening to music could be redirected by teaching him to play a simple percussion instrument in the high school band. Julie's interest in electronic games could lead to teaching her to use a computer with CD Rom. John could readily be taught to play an interactive game like "Hungry Hippo," by teaching the related skills of play, such as getting out the pieces, asking others to play and recognizing when the game is finished.

Note Dan's updated Leisure Lifestyle Profile which reflects his expanded leisure pattern and competencies after the *Exposure Component*. The profile shows his level of independence in the leisure activity and related skills for each activity that he participates in. Dan's Leisure Lifestyle Profile shows that he now has several activities that he does alone at home, but only one that he does with anyone else. He needs assistance to develop additional interests and skills for activities that he does at home with his parents, friends or caregivers. This can be developed through the systematic exposure (*Exposure Component*) to age-appropriate activities of potential interest to both Dan and his leisure partners.

Dan has a limited number of things that he does alone in the community or school. Due to the nature of Dan's disabilities, he is seldom alone in the community, at work or at school. However, he still needs to be able to occupy free time by himself in these environments at times such as homeroom, break, and lunch. Partial participation is an excellent strategy, but at least some activities should be identified that he can do independently. Rather than adding more activities, many activities can be expanded into other environments. For instance, listening to a stereo cassette would be potentially appropriate in all three environments for Dan.

The development of all the related leisure skills for independence becomes a major focus once there are preferred activities in each grid. The completed profile provides information for prioritizing necessary related skills for instruction. In general, it appears that Dan needs focused training on making choices, on initiating activities and on social interaction between activities. He also needs training on social interaction during activities, such as asking others to do an activity with him and engaging in a basic conversational routine. With this additional training, his playing "Hoop" basketball alone at home might be expanded to his playing basketball with co-workers during breaks at work and during lunch at school.

Although he is relatively independent with his cassette recorder, he could become more independent with his music. His visual impairment makes it difficult for him to identify his tapes, but he can identify a few tapes through smell. Teaching him a system to help him identify and organize his cassettes would increase his independence. He also could be more involved in choosing and purchasing his own music, since music stores often play samples of music for prospective buyers.

As the individual with autism gains more activity and related skills, other variables may be addressed, such as the variety of types of activities, activity levels and environments. Dan's community participation needs to be expanded. One focus for Dan might be to expand solitary community activities. Swimming and weight lifting are individual sports that are possibilities for him. Getting him an adapted aquatics card so that community pools would allow him to swim alone is a possible goal. Elective classes such as band and woodworking and extracurricular activities can be new outlets for him. He is meeting new friends in woodworking and other elective classes.

LEISURE LIFESTYLE PROFILE

| Student | Dan | Date: | May 1, 1997 |

ACTIVITY	Id Time	Resources	Choice	Initiate	Skills	Interact	Problem Solve	COMMENTS
HOME (Activity within property boundaries of home or personal space)								
Alone								
Exercise Bike	I	I	I	I	I	NA	NA	
Mini Tramp	I	I	I	I	I	NA	NA	
Stereo Cassette	I	E	E	I	I	NA	TA	
Hoop (Basketball)	I	E	I	I	E	NA	NA	
With Others								
Stereo Cassette with mom	E	I	E	I	I	E	TA	
COMMUNITY (Activity beyond property boundaries of home)								
Alone								
With Others								
Walking	PA	I	E	I	I	E	TA	
Bowling	PA	TA	TA	E	PA	E	TA	
Swimming	TA	E	TA	PS	E	E	TA	
SCHOOL/WORK (Activity during recess, breaks, lunch, elective classes and extracurricular activities)								
Alone								
Talking Books	E	TA	E	E	E	NA	TA	
With Others								
Jogging (P.E.)	PA	E	E	E	E	E	PA	
Hoop/Catch	PA	E	I	E	E	E	I	
Woodworking	PA	E	E	E	PA	E	PA	
Assemblies	PA	E	E	E	E	E	E	

Record enjoyed activities engaged in for at least 15 minutes, 12 times a year.
Enter the appropriate code using the following:

I	=	Independently completes without cue, or prompt.
E	=	Emerging; knows what the activity is about, or can partially complete it without adaptations.
PA	=	Participates with adaptations at predetermined level.
TA	=	Total assistance needed to complete.
NA	=	Not applicable; not required in activity, or unconventional activity in which skill is not defined.

Community Referenced Activities

Every community has different opportunities for leisure in home, school, work and community. To make training for a leisure activity worthwhile, the individual must have continued opportunities for participation in the activity after training. Methods for identifying viable leisure activities are covered in Chapter 3: Assessment.

Ongoing Assessment

Assessment of the individual's progress needs to be an ongoing process and serve as the basis for changes in training strategies. The Leisure Lifestyle Profile presented in Chapter 3 provides a form to record progress and note needed modifications. When an individual is not making progress or is having frequent behavior problems, some element of the training sequence or environment needs to be modified. Sometimes a very small change in instruction or the environment will make a major difference. Indications during training that an activity is not preferred and should probably be discontinued are a lack of progress, despite systematic efforts to modify instruction, and a failure to select the trained activity when given a choice.

Summary

Training involves a major commitment of time and resources. Pre-planning and preparing is necessary. Two essential elements in designing leisure training programs for individuals with autism are the appropriate choice of leisure activities and the selection of effective training procedures. Although individuals with autism have many common difficulties and characteristics related to leisure participation, it is important to establish specific individualized objectives and identify appropriate training strategies.

Sometimes the same activities are presented in the *Exposure Component* as in the *Training Component*. *Exposure* gives the individual with autism some understanding and experience with the activity. *Training* is designed to develop the leisure activity and related skills to be as competent as possible in the activity.

The Components presented provide a framework to assess and develop interests, as well as to identify necessary areas for training in the leisure domain. It is hoped that a clear differentiation of these elements will help in the development of more specific and individualized program plan objectives and, thereby, more meaningful leisure participation.

Appendices

Appendix A
Typical Leisure Behavior & Age-Appropriate Activities Lists

1. Typical Leisure/Play Behaviors & Interests: Birth to Adolescence
2. Age-Appropriate Activities List: Ages 5 to 8
3. Age-Appropriate Activities List: Ages 9 to 12
4. Age-Appropriate Activities List: Ages 13 to 15
5. Age-Appropriate Activities List: Ages 16 +

Appendix B
Directions & Forms for Leisure Assessment

1. Directions for Leisure Lifestyle Profile
2. Leisure Lifestyle Profile (blank)
3. Leisure Behavior Questionnaire (blank)
4. Directions for Leisure Observation Sheet
5. Leisure Observation Sheet (blank)
6. Leisure Interest Inventory for Friends & Family (blank)
7. Leisure Interest Survey (blank)
8. Directions for Natural Settings & Resources for Activities
9. Natural Settings & Resources for Activities (blank)

Appendix C
Activity Cards

1. Activity Card Index
2. Activity Cards & Descriptions
3. Blank Assessment Card

Appendix D
Discrepancy Analysis with Hypothesis

1. Directions for Discrepancy Analysis with Hypothesis
2. Discrepancy Analysis with Hypothesis (blank)

Appendix A

Typical Leisure Behavior and Age-Appropriate Activities Lists

TYPICAL LEISURE/PLAY BEHAVIORS and INTERESTS: BIRTH - ADOLESCENCE

DEVELOPMENTAL AGE	Birth - 6 months	7 - 12 months	13 - 18 months	Variable	19 - 24 months
CHARACTERISTICS	Orienting: mouths, licks, bites, body moves, babbles, vocal patterns	Repetitive manual manipulation	EXPLORATORY	Observing behaviors of others	Repetitious: Pulling, pounding, throwing, jumping, climbing (locomotor exploration)
		PRACTICE (FUNCTIONAL) PLAY			
		NON-INTERACTIVE			
SOCIAL INTERACTION	Unoccupied behavior	Solitary independent		Onlooker	Parallel
# PARTICIPANTS	1	1	1	Variable	Variable
EXAMPLES OF ACTIVITIES AND MATERIALS	Senses and body; other bodies, concrete objects, soft cuddly toys, mobile for crib, noisemakers, large plastic rings, etc.		Peek-a-book, Where's Baby?, Patty Cake, Treasure Hunt, This Little Piggy, Eeentsie Weentsie Spider, Horsey, etc. Squeaky play animals, unbreakable dolls, empty containers with removable lids, floating bath animals, nests of hollow blocks or boxes, etc.		Water play, sand play Crayons, 3-5 piece puzzle, large ball, tom-tom, wagon, rocking horse, pull toys, pound toys, pots, pans, wooden spoons, large containers, sponges, etc.

TYPICAL LEISURE/PLAY BEHAVIORS and INTERESTS: BIRTH - ADOLESCENCE

DEVELOPMENTAL AGE	2 - 3 years	3 - 4 years	4 - 5 years	5 - 6 years
CHARACTERISTICS	*Investigatory: climbing, running, jumping, digging; no give and take in play*	*Representative, imaginary; climbing, swinging, role play*	*Make believe play; cooking with parent; takes turns, shares toys*	*Systematic: varied construction; conforms, some rivalry, increased doll play*
		PRE-OPERATIONAL (SYMBOLIC) PLAY		
		INTERACTIVE		
SOCIAL INTERACTION	*Associative play*	*Cooperative play* One-to-one	*Cooperative play* One-to-others	*Cooperative play* Group
# PARTICIPANTS	2 or 3	1:1	2 or 3	2 - 5
EXAMPLES OF ACTIVITIES AND MATERIALS	*Not yet ready for organized games Dress up, telephone play* *Bean bags, housekeeping equipment, costume box, hollow blocks, large wooden beads, picture books, push-pull toys*	*Singing games (Here we Go Round the Mulberry Bush)* *Bubble set, clay, sand, farm and zoo animal sets, costume box for dress up clothes, floor blocks with family figures, transportation play materials, steering wheel, large cartons, hammer and nails*	*Hide and seek, tag, red rover, sewing cards, King on the Mountain* *Finger paints, crayons, blunt scissors and paste, puppets, play luggage, housekeeping equipment, wood scraps, Play Doh*	*Simple circle games (Duck Duck Goose), jump rope, hopscotch, target toss, bat ball* *8-20 piece puzzles, puppets, play circus, fix-it and try-it materials, tricycle and bicycle, stacking and nesting toys, plants*

TYPICAL LEISURE/PLAY BEHAVIORS and INTERESTS: BIRTH - ADOLESCENCE

DEVELOPMENTAL AGE	6 - 8 years	8 - 10 years	10 years and up
CHARACTERISTICS	Construction, wrestling and tussling, curious about nature	Preoccupation with realism; operational, like friends of own sex	Specialization of interests (hobbies, collections); yield to group, team spirit
	CONCRETE OPERATIONS	FORMAL OPERATIONS	
	INTERACTIVE		
SOCIAL INTERACTION	Group	Cooperative team	Competitive team
# PARTICIPANTS	2+	Variable	Variable
EXAMPLES OF ACTIVITIES AND MATERIALS	Low organized games (Steal the Bacon); not ready for team activities in which the group wins rather than the individual. Checkers; target games	Lead up games (Newcombe) and relays; clubs; writing to pen pals	Regular sports with adult rules adapted to needs (tennis, basketball); news and poetry writing; band and orchestra; choral groups; social dances, creative dramatics
	Plaster of Paris, papier mache, table games (lotto, Parcheesi), wagon, jump rope, marbles, pogo stick, kite, playhouse, puppets, boy & girl dolls, climbing apparatus, chalk board, clay, nature crafts, nature games	Steam engines, electro-magnets, old alarm clocks, sports equipment, bicycle skates, craft sets, hobby sets, live pets, table games, table games (Chinese Checkers), box hockey, table tennis	Hobby sets, musical instruments, camera, sports equipment, electrical and scientific equipment, books of reference, tools, character dolls and materials for making doll clothes, record player, table games (chess, Dominos, poker, etc.)

Age-Appropriate Activities List
Ages 5-8

Leisure/Recreation

2.1 Media	2.2 Exercise	2.3 Games/Crafts/Hobbies	2.4 Events	2.5 Other
2.1.1 Listening to radio	2.2.1 Playground play	2.3.1 Playing video/computer games	2.4.1 Having/going to parties	2.5.1 Spending time with friends
2.1.2 Using cassette/CD player	2.2.2 Climbing trees	2.3.2 Playing table/board games	2.4.2 Participating in special holidays	2.5.2 Spending night with friend/having or attending a slumber party
2.1.3 Watching TV	2.2.3 Riding bike/scooter	2.3.3 Playing cards	2.4.3 Attending/participating in school events/meetings	2.5.3 Car camping
2.1.4 Using VCR	2.2.4 Jumping rope	2.3.4 Playing with toys		
2.1.5 Watching home movies/slides	2.2.5 Using stationary exercise machines	2.3.5 Playing Velcro darts	2.4.4 Attending Scout/4H meetings	2.5.4 Visiting relatives
2.1.6 Using telephone answering machine	2.2.6 Jogging/running in road races	2.3.6 Doing puzzles	2.4.5 Going to fairs/festivals	2.5.5 Attending Church/Temple services & events
2.1.7 Reading books/magazines/newspapers	2.2.7 Playing catch/frisbee	2.3.7 Creating art projects, ex. -coloring -painting -ceramics -attending community arts & crafts class	2.4.6 Going to craft fairs	2.5.6 Going to the zoo, planetarium, museum, aquarium
	2.2.8 Playing ball games; ex. T-ball, basketball, soccer, 4-square, keep-away		2.4.7 Going to library activities/community events for children	
2.1.8 Listening to stories				
	2.2.9 Participating on team athletic events	2.3.8 Collecting (coins, stamps, stickers, trading cards, rocks, etc.)	2.4.8 Going to flea markets/garage sales	
	2.2.10 Roller skating			
	2.2.11 Swimming	2.3.9 Making/flying kites, paper airplanes, gliders	2.4.9 Going to the movies	
	2.2.12 Hiking			
	2.2.13 Fishing	2.3.10 Singing	2.4.10 Attending/performing in cultural performances: concerts, plays, dances, etc.	
	2.2.14 Boating/rafting	2.3.11 Playing a musical instrument		
	2.2.15 Skiing (water, snow)			
	2.2.16 Horseback riding		2.4.11 Attending sports events	
	2.2.17 Dancing lessons		2.4.12 Attending other events with family	
	2.2.18 Yoga			
	2.2.19 Gymnastics class			

From *Elementary/Secondary System*. Used with permission by Diane Ferguson, Specialized training Program, University of Oregon, Eugene, OR.

Age-Appropriate Activities List
Ages 9-12

Leisure/Recreation

2.1 Media	2.2 Exercise	2.3 Games/Crafts/Hobbies	2.4 Events	2.5 Other
2.1.1 Listening to radio	2.2.1 Using parks/playgrounds	2.3.1 Playing video/computer games	2.4.1 Having/going to parties	2.5.1 Spending time with friends
2.1.2 Using cassette/CD player	2.2.2 Climbing trees	2.3.2 Playing table/board games	2.4.2 Participating in special holidays	2.5.2 Spending night with friend/having or attending a slumber party
2.1.3 Watching TV	2.2.3 Riding bike/scooter	2.3.3 Playing cards	2.4.3 Attending/participating in school events/meetings	
2.1.4 Using VCR	2.2.4 Skate boarding	2.3.4 Playing billiards		
2.1.5 Watching home movies/slides	2.2.5 Jumping rope	2.3.5 Playing darts		2.5.3 Car camping
2.1.6 Using telephone answering machine	2.2.6 Using stationary exercise machines	2.3.6 Doing puzzles	2.4.4 Attending Scout/4H/Club meetings	2.5.4 Visiting relatives
2.1.7 Reading books/magazines/newspapers	2.2.7 Jogging/running in road races/Track & Field events	2.3.7 Creating art projects, ex. -drawing -painting -calligraphy -ceramics -attending community arts & crafts class	2.4.5 Going to fairs/festivals/exhibits	2.5.5 Attending Church/Temple services & events
	2.2.8 Playing catch/frisbee		2.4.6 Going to craft fairs/markets	2.5.6 Going to the zoo, planetarium, museum, aquarium
	2.2.9 Playing ball games; ex. T-ball, basketball, soccer, 4-square, keep-away, football, etc.	2.3.8 Needle crafts: ex. sewing, knitting, weaving, crocheting, leatherwork	2.4.7 Going to/participating in community events for kids/teens/fanmilies	
	2.2.10 Playing racquet games: tennis, badminton, ping pong, etc.	2.3.9 Woodworking, metal work, stained glass	2.4.8 Going to flea markets/garage sales	
	2.2.11 Golfing/mini-golf	2.3.10 Jewelry making	2.4.9 Going to the movies	
	2.2.12 Participating on team athletic events	2.3.11 Collecting (coins, stamps, stickers. stickers, trading cards, rocks, etc.)	2.4.10 Attending/performing in cultural performances: concerts, plays, dances, lectures, etc.	
	2.2.13 Karate/wrestling			
	2.2.14 Bowling	2.3.12 Taking photographs/using a video camera		
	2.2.15 Roller blading/skating; ice skating			
	2.2.16 Swimming/diving	2.3.13 Making a photo album, scrapbook	2.4.11 Attending sports events	
	2.2.17 Hiking/climbing	2.3.14 Making/flying kites, paper airplanes, gliders	2.4.12 Attending other events: ex. monster truck rallies, car races, animal shows, air shows, etc.	
	2.2.18 Camping			
	2.2.19 Fishing/hunting			
	2.2.20 Boating/rafting	2.3.15 Building models		
	2.2.21 Skiing (water, snow)	2.3.16 Singing		
	2.2.22 Horseback riding	2.3.17 Playing a musical instrument		
	2.2.23 Dancing lessons	2.3.18 Having a pen pal		
	2.2.24 Yoga	2.3.19 Using a chemistry set/running science experiments		
	2.2.25 Gymnastics class			
	2.2.26 Doing aerobics (class, video tape)	2.3.20 Learning a foreign language		
	2.2.27 Weight lifting			

Age-Appropriate Activities List
Ages 13-15

Leisure/Recreation

2.1 Media	2.2 Exercise	2.3 Games/Crafts/Hobbies	2.4 Events	2.5 Other
2.1.1 Listening to radio	2.2.1 Using parks	2.3.1 Playing video/computer games	2.4.1 Having/going to parties	2.5.1 Spending time with friends
2.1.2 Using cassette/CD player	2.2.2 Climbing trees	2.3.2 Playing table/board games	2.4.2 Participating in special holidays	2.5.2 Spending night with friend/having or attending a slumber party
2.1.3 Watching TV	2.2.3 Riding bike/scooter	2.3.3 Playing cards	2.4.3 Attending/participating in school events/meetings	
2.1.4 Using VCR	2.2.4 Skate boarding	2.3.4 Playing billiards		2.5.3 Going on dates
2.1.5 Watching home movies/slides	2.2.5 Jumping rope	2.3.5 Playing darts		2.5.4 Car camping
	2.2.6 Using stationary exercise machines	2.3.6 Doing puzzles	2.4.4 Attending Scout/4H/Club meetings	2.5.5 Visiting relatives
2.1.6 Using telephone answering machine	2.2.7 Jogging/running in road races/Track & Field events	2.3.7 Creating art projects, ex. -drawing -painting -calligraphy -ceramics -attending community arts & crafts class	2.4.5 Going to fairs/festivals/exhibits	2.5.6 Attending Church/Temple services & events
2.1.7 Reading books/magazines/newspapers			2.4.6 Going to craft fairs/markets	2.5.7 Going to the zoo, planetarium, museum, aquarium
	2.2.8 Playing catch/frisbee		2.4.7 Going to/participating in community events for teens/fanmilies	
	2.2.9 Playing ball games; ex. hackey-sack, basketball, soccer, football etc.			
	2.2.10 Playing racquet games: tennis, badminton, ping pong, etc.	2.3.8 Needle crafts: ex. sewing, knitting, weaving, crocheting, leatherwork		
	2.2.11 Golfing	2.3.9 Woodworking, metal work, stained glass	2.4.8 Going to flea markets/garage sales	
	2.2.12 Participating on team athletic events			
	2.2.13 Karate/wrestling	2.3.10 Jewelry making	2.4.9 Going to the movies	
	2.2.14 Bowling	2.3.11 Collecting (coins, stamps, stickers. stickers, trading cards, rocks, etc.)	2.4.10 Attending/performing in cultural performances: concerts, plays, dances, lectures, etc.	
	2.2.15 Roller blading/skating; ice skating			
	2.2.16 Swimming/diving/surfing	2.3.12 Taking photographs/using a video camera		
	2.2.17 Hiking/climbing	2.3.13 Making a photo album, scrapbook	2.4.11 Attending sports events	
	2.2.18 Running circuits: adventure courses	2.3.14 Making/flying kites, paper airplanes, gliders	2.4.12 Attending other events: ex. monster truck rallies, car races, animal shows, air shows, etc.	
	2.2.19 Camping			
	2.2.20 Fishing/hunting	2.3.15 Building models		
	2.2.21 Boating/rafting	2.3.16 Singing		
	2.2.22 Skiing (water, snow); snowboarding/sledding	2.3.17 Playing a musical instrument		
		2.3.18 Having a pen pal		
	2.2.23 Horseback riding	2.3.19 Using a chemistry set/running science experiments		
	2.2.24 Dancing lessons			
	2.2.25 Yoga			
	2.2.26 Gymnastics class	2.3.20 Learning a foreign language		
	2.2.27 Doing aerobics (class, video tape)			
	2.2.28 Weight lifting			

Age-Appropriate Activities List
Ages 16+

Leisure

2.1 Exercise	2.2 Games/ Crafts/ Hobbies	2.3 Events	2.4 Media	2.5 Other
2.1.1 Walking	2.2.1 Playing computer games	2.3.1 Attending Club meetings	2.4.1 Reading newspapers/ magazines/books	2.5.1 Talking with friends /family on the telephone
2.1.2 Jogging	2.2.2 Playing video games	2.3.2 Using the library	2.4.2 Listening to the radio	2.5.2 Maintaining intimate relationships
2.1.3 Riding a bike	2.2.3 Playing hand-held video games	2.3.3 Attending community events	2.4.3 Using a cassette player	2.5.3 Visiting family/ friends
2.1.4 Playing catch	2.2.4 Playing card games		2.4.4 Listening to talking books	2.5.4 Using a whirlpool steam room/ hot tub/sauna
2.1.5 Attending Skill-Building classes	2.2.5 Playing table games		2.4.5 Playing records	
2.1.6 Swimming	2.2.6 Working puzzles		2.4.6 Using a VCR	2.5.5 Using a tanning salon/sunbathing
2.1.7 Participating in Aerobics/ Slimnastics/ Jazzercise class	2.2.7 Doing needle crafts		2.4.7 Using a Viewmaster	2.5.6 Going out dancing
2.1.8 Using exercise equipment	2.2.8 Golf		2.4.8 Watching television	2.5.7 Going to a bar/ tavern
2.1.9 Weight training	2.2.9 Playing darts			
2.1.10 Playing racquet sports	2.2.10 Shooting pool			
2.1.11 Skating	2.2.11 Playing an instrument			
2.1.12 Skateboarding	2.2.12 Building a collection			
2.1.13 Participating in dance classes	2.2.13 Flying a kite/ model plane			
2.1.14 Playing team sports	2.2.14 Playing lawn games			
2.1.15 Being a Team Manager	2.2.15 Attending art/ craft classes			
2.1.16 Golfing	2.2.16 Doing miscellaneous art projects			
2.1.17 Horseback riding	2.2.17 Weaving/doing fiber arts			
2.1.18 Hiking/ backpacking	2.2.18 Woodworking			
2.1.19 Snow shoeing	2.2.19 Gardening			
2.1.20 Skiing	2.2.20 Fishing/hunting			
2.1.21 Boating				

Appendix B

Directions and Forms for Leisure Assessment

Directions for Leisure Lifestyle Profile

Description of the Leisure Lifestyle Profile

The Leisure Lifestyle Profile offers an overview of the individual's present leisure pattern and skills. It is designed as a tool for planning individualized leisure education programs.

Directions

Identify activities that the individual performs for a minimum of fifteen minutes, at least twelve times a year. List activities in the appropriate grids for location (home, community, work/school) and level of social interaction (alone or with others).

Rate each of the following related leisure skills in the appropriate columns using the key on the bottom of the Leisure Lifestyle Profile:

ID Time: Identification of free time for engaging in preferred activities.

Resources: Identification and utilization of necessary equipment, attire, money and resources for activity.

Choice: Selection of activity.

Initiate: Self-initiation of the activity.

Skills: Demonstration of skills necessary for participation in the activity.

Interact: Demonstration of social interaction skills required for the activity.

Problem Solve: Demonstration of problem-solving skills related to participation in the activity.

Interpreting the Leisure Lifestyle Profile

The Profile provides much useful information on the nature of the individual's leisure skills and pattern. It offers a view of the present balance of activities in different settings and in solitary situations compared to social situations.

The ultimate goal is that the individual has the related leisure skills to actively choose and engage in a variety of activities in a variety of environments. An initial goal is a minimum of one activity in each grid. For an individual without activities in each grid, initial planning usually includes expanding leisure interests and skills for a better balance. This may be developed through systematic exposure to age-appropriate activities of potential interest. Although social interaction is an important goal, the individual, also, needs some solitary activities. The greatest amount of free time is generally spent at home, so a higher number of activities at home is appropriate. Partial participation is an excellent strategy; however, some activities should be identified that the individual can do independently.

Once there are preferred activities in each grid, the development of all related leisure skills necessary for independence becomes a major focus. The profile provides information for prioritizing necessary related skills for instruction. Rather than adding more activities, many activities may also be expanded to other environments. As the individual grasps more activities and related skills, other variables may be addressed as well, such as variety in types of activities, activity levels, etc.

For more on leisure assessment and the Leisure Lifestyle Profile, see Chapter 3.

LEISURE LIFESTYLE PROFILE

Student: _____ **Date:** _____

ACTIVITY	Id Time	Resources	Choice	Initiate	Skills	Interact	Problem Solve	COMMENTS
HOME (Activity within property boundaries of home or personal space)								
Alone								
With Others								
COMMUNITY (Activity beyond property boundaries of home)								
Alone								
With Others								
SCHOOL/WORK (Activity during recess, breaks, lunch, elective classes and extracurricular activities)								
Alone								
With Others								

Record enjoyed activities engaged in for at least 15 minutes, 12 times a year.
Enter the appropriate code using the following:

I	=	Independently completes without cue, or prompt.
E	=	Emerging; knows what the activity is about, or can partially complete it without adaptations.
PA	=	Participates with adaptations at predetermined level.
TA	=	Total assistance needed to complete.
NA	=	Not applicable; not required in activity, or unconventional activity in which skill is not defined.

LEISURE BEHAVIOR QUESTIONNAIRE

CHILD'S NAME	AGE	RESPONDENT'S NAME	DATE

INSTRUCTIONS: Please list activities as indicated and rate your child on each of the leisure activities. Be sure to fill in all of the appropriate squares. After completing Section "A", please provide information for each of the additional questions in Sections "B" and "C".

A. Please list up to five (5) activities that your child enjoys in each category and fill in the squares for each activity. Example: If you listed computer games under "Games/Crafts/Hobbies" as an activity that your child plays at least once a week, and does as well as peers, you would enter:

PARTICIPATION			AMOUNT OF INVOLVEMENT		LEVEL OF SKILL				
Involved at least 1 time/wk.	Involved at least 1 time/mth.	Involved 2-3 times/yr.	Observes	Participates	None	Low	Average	High	Not Known
■	☐	☐	☐	■	☐	☐	■	☐	☐

1. Media (e.g., cassette/CD player, radio, magazines)

a. _____
b. _____
c. _____
d. _____
e. _____

2. Exercise (e.g., swims, plays catch/Frisbee, hikes)

a. _____
b. _____
c. _____
d. _____
e. _____

3. Games/Crafts/Hobbies (e.g., computer games, puzzles, collections, printing)

a. _____
b. _____
c. _____
d. _____
e. _____

4. Events (e.g., parties, fairs, movies, concerts)

a. _____
b. _____
c. _____
d. _____
e. _____

5. Other (e.g., socializing, youth groups, museums)

a. _____
b. _____
c. _____
d. _____
e. _____

B. Please answer the following questions about your child. If you have a response which is not noted, please use the 'other' category to respond.

1. My child spends the majority of his/her free time:
   ☐ alone
   ☐ watching others
   ☐ playing beside people without interaction
   ☐ interacting with others on a similar activity
   ☐ sharing and cooperating in play
   ☐ other _____ (specify)

2. During free time, my child will usually:
   ☐ do nothing
   ☐ only participate when activities are initiated by others
   ☐ spontaneously initiate activity
   ☐ indicate need for assistance
   ☐ seek a playmate or friend
   ☐ plan an activity
   ☐ other _____ (specify)

3. My child usually participates in activities located at
   ☐ home
   ☐ park or playground
   ☐ home
   ☐ school
   ☐ neighbor's home
   ☐ general community
   ☐ other _____ (specify)

C. Please give your thoughts on the following:

1. List up to five leisure activities that you personally enjoy doing:
   a. _____
   b. _____
   c. _____
   d. _____
   e. _____

2. How does your family usually spend its vacation?

3. List up to five leisure activities in which you might like to see your child engaged in the future:
   a. _____
   b. _____
   c. _____
   d. _____
   e. _____

4. List any difficulties that you feel your child has in getting involved in leisure activities:
   a. _____
   b. _____
   c. _____
   d. _____
   e. _____

Thank you for your assistance.

Directions for Leisure Observation Sheet

Preparation

Set up a recreation area with at least six items which provide an opportunity for different types of use and interaction. For example, a magazine would provide an opportunity for solitary activity, whereas a ball would provide opportunity for social interaction. The area should be arranged so that different types of activities, such as table activities and physical activity can occur.

Explain that this is free time and that the individual can do what s/he wants in that area. Avoid direct participation in an activity unless involvement is requested by the individual.

Recording Information

After an adjustment period of at least five minutes, observations of behaviors are recorded on the Leisure Observation Sheet in four consecutive five-minute periods. The five-minute intervals can be signaled by a timer. Initially, four to six days of observations are often necessary to get adequate information. Three areas are covered in coding: social level, social interactions, and activity involvement.

Place a mark under the appropriate social level during each five-minute interval using the following code:

Watches Others: exhibits no behavior other than as an onlooker; is aware of others and is observing them

No Activity: unoccupied behavior, such as staring into space or self-stimulation, such as rocking; no contact with an external object or another person

Plays Alone: plays alone with an object that is different than those used by peers within close proximity

Plays Beside Peers: approximates the action of one or more peers, but does not interact

Interacts With Peers: interacts with peers doing same or similar activity; includes borrowing or loaning equipment

Engages in Cooperative Play: mutually interacts with peers in doing an activity; activity can not continue without cooperation, e.g.. playing catch or checkers.

Record all social interactions during each five-minute interval under the Social Interactions section of the Leisure Observation Sheet. Describe materials selected and how they are used.

LEISURE OBSERVATION SHEET

CODE BEHAVIORS FOR FOUR CONSECUTIVE FIVE-MINUTE PERIODS DURING UNSTRUCTURED TIME.

Name:
Date:
Time:
School:
Observer:

Describe Activity (object involved, other people involved, place, behavior, etc.)				
SOCIAL INTERACTIONS				
Continues to Interact with Peer				
Continues to Interact with Adult				
Initiates to Peer				
Initiates to Adult				
Responds to Peer				
Responds to Adult				
No Response to Peers				
No Response to Adult				
SOCIAL LEVEL				
Interacts with Adult Only				
Engages in Cooperative Activity				
Interacts with Peers in Play				
Plays Beside Peers				
Plays Alone				
No Activity				
Watches Others				

LEISURE INTEREST INVENTORY
for
FRIENDS and FAMILY

Name: _____   **Date:** _____

Directions: The purpose of this inventory is to determine the types of activities that you enjoy doing. It will, also, be used to identify possible leisure opportunities for your friend. Please take the time to think about your own leisure and complete this inventory.

1. **List what you do for enjoyment or relaxation.**
   - When you get home from school or work:
   - After dinner:
   - During break times at school or work:
   - During lunch:

2. **What do you like to do for exercise or fitness?**

3. **List clubs or groups in which you participate:**

   - _____   - _____
   - _____   - _____
   - _____   - _____
   - _____   - _____

4. **List classes you have taken for fun in the last two years:**

   - _____   - _____
   - _____   - _____
   - _____   - _____
   - _____   - _____

5. **List some activities you enjoy doing.**
   With your family:

   - _____   - _____
   - _____   - _____
   - _____   - _____
   - _____   - _____

   With your family:

   - _____   - _____
   - _____   - _____
   - _____   - _____
   - _____   - _____

LEISURE INTEREST SURVEY

NAME: DATE: AGE:

EXERCISE/ ACTIVITY	Do you enjoy it?	Did you do it in the last month?	How often?	Does anyone else in the family do it?	Where did you do it?	Who do you do it with?	Would you like to do it with your special friend?	COMMENTS

Comments:

Directions for Natural Settings and Resources for Activities Form

Description

The Natural Settings & Resources for Activities Form provides a community-referenced list of age-appropriate activities with a list of where the activities commonly occur or are available. It was developed to identify natural settings and resources for activities in communities for individuals of various ages. It is a tool to identify potential leisure activities for inclusion on individualized plans, to determine natural settings for instruction and to identify other places for generalization of leisure skills.

Procedure

Make a list of potential activities. The Age-Appropriate Activities List located in Appendix A is a good source of potential activities. Survey where these activities are available in your community and indicate availability on the Natural Settings & Resources for Activities Form.

The Natural Settings & Resources for Activities Form is divided into three major environments: school, home and community. The school section includes the times when there are naturally-occurring opportunities to learn or participate in leisure activities: break/between classes, recess, extracurricular activities, and elective classes. the community section includes the places or agencies that offer this activity. List specific clubs and types of commercial facilities. The home section includes whether the activity is done inside the house or outside in the yard or neighborhood.

NATURAL SETTINGS & RESOURCES FOR ACTIVITIES

			LEISURE ACTIVITIES
HOME		Inside	
		Outside	
COMMUNITY		Commercial Recreation	
		Clubs/ Organizations	
		Community Colleges	
	Parks Department		
		Recreation Programs	
		Parks/ Playgrounds	
SCHOOL		Elective Classes/ Specials	
		Extracurricular	
		Recess	
		Break/Between Classes	

Appendix C

Activity Cards

Activity Card Index

Please refer to Chapter 5 for information on the format
and use of the Activity Cards.

Community/Social Activities 95

    The Zoo
    Bowling
    In the Park
    What's to Eat?
    Swimming
    Fish, Oh Boy!!
    Let's Call a Friend

Games 133

    Mr. Mouth
    Uno Cards
    Lotto
    Family and Friends Lotto
    War Cards
    Sorry®
    Candyland Bingo

Sports 151

    Hopping Along
    Lawn Darts
    Obstacle Course
    On the Line 1
    On the Line 2
    Basketball
    Roller Skates

Hobbies/Crafts 165

    Where Does It Go??
    Growing Ideas: Eggheads
    Growing Ideas: Growing Plants
    Scrappy Ideas
    Modeling Away
    Jewelry/Earring Making
    Listening to Music: Audio Books
    Listening to Music: Cassette Music
    Making Music

Hobbies/Arts 187

    Painting: Finger Painting
    Painting: Shirt Painting
    * Pottery: Pinch Pots
    * Pottery: Candle Holders
    * Pottery: Coil Pots
    * Pottery: Wind Chimes
    Stuff It In

Other Activities...............................203

    What Goes There?
    Flapping in the Wind
    What Does It Feel Like?
    Squishy Squashy Fun
    Stick It On
    Where Does It Go?

Blank Activity Assessment Card....217

    * Baker's Clay Recipe 219

Community / Social Activity Cards

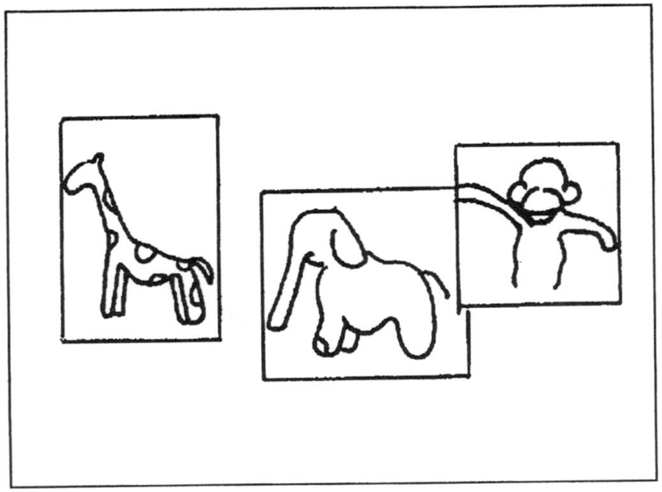

THE ZOO (Get Ready)

Why Are We Doing This?
To allow the child to begin planning, organizing and anticipating a trip to the zoo. This will help reduce anxiety and confusion.

Materials:
Pictures of zoo animals
Plastic zoo animals
Large sheets of paper
Pens

General Rule of Thumb:
1. Review with objects and pictures what the zoo looks like and what kind of animals live there. Remember these children learn from a natural context or the real thing. They will respond better if they can anticipate what will happen.
2. Draw a map of the zoo on a large sheet of paper.
3. Place pictures/objects on the map in the appropriate areas.
4. Move around your map, first go see the elephants, then the tigers, etc.
5. Will you take a lunch? See menu planning card, meal preparation, and packing up card.

Choices:
Present as many choices as possible, for example, which animal would you like to see first? third? Which zoo story do you want to hear? Which animals on the map do you want to see?

Do It Yourself:
Encourage asking questions. What is it? Where do we go now? Practice the language they may need to help independence there as you do on your map.

And Furthermore:
This activity can expand to one goal a day in preparation. The first day categorize the animals, taking time to find pictures, objects, songs, stories. The second day review the zoo map and repeat the labels, songs, and stories. Also don't forget the language opportunities. Label for the child what they are seeing and hearing.

Activity Story

I will be going to the zoo on _____. Today I will plan our trip.

I will find pictures of animals that live in the zoo. I will draw a map of where the animals live in the zoo.

I may go to the zoo with my family or with friends. I will stay by whoever I go with. This is one rule.

There is a train at the zoo. If I want to ride the train I will tell who I am with.

I will think about the animals I will see. I will think about what I will see or hear at the zoo.

In _____ days I will go to the zoo.

1. Get Materials

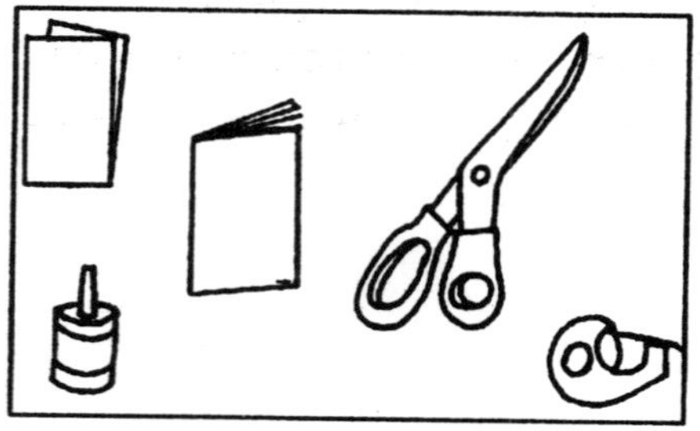

2. Find pictures of animals that live in the zoo.

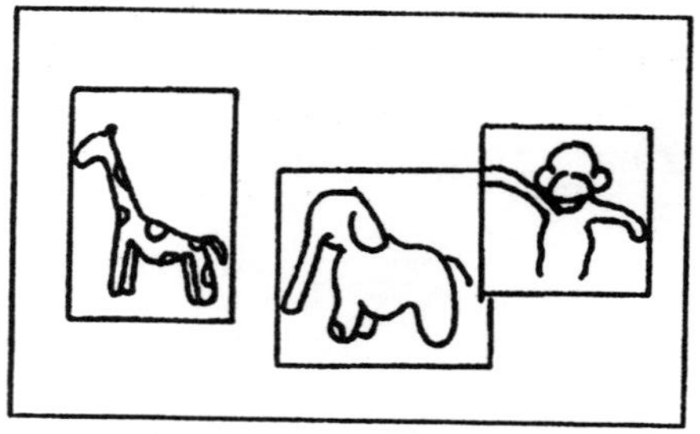

3. Draw a map of the zoo. Put animals in it.

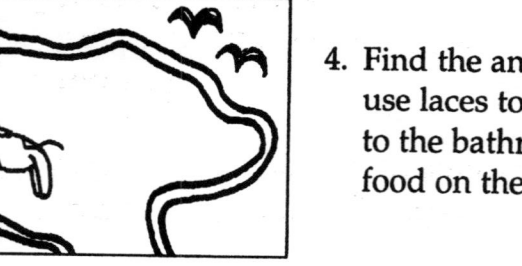

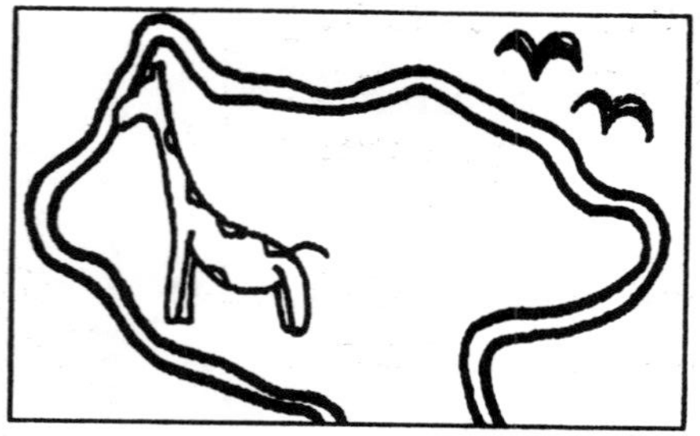

4. Find the animals, maybe use laces to show the paths to the bathroom or to get food on the map.

THE ZOO (The Real Thing)

Why Are We Doing This?
FUN!! Exposure to real life animals.

Materials:
Money for admission and/or snack
Prepared picnic lunch

General Rule Of Thumb:
1. Do preparation activity first.
2. Get there safely. Practice and review rules for the zoo. (i.e. stay with buddy, etc.)
3. Allow the child, within reason, to set the amount of time to view each animal.
4. There are plenty of opportunities to practice language skills. "What do you see?" "What are they doing?"
5. Take a break. Practice ordering a snack or eat the lunch you have prepared (see lunch preparation).
6. Be sure to give the child adequate warning for when it will be time to go. "We will see the penguins and then we will leave."

Choices:
As mentioned, allow the child to determine how long to stay at each animal. If you order a snack or drink let the child choose what he/she wants.

Do It Yourself:
Encourage the child to ask questions.

And Furthermore:
Practice language skills such as labeling. You might want to bring along the pictures or objects you used in the preparation activity to relate to what they are seeing in person.

Cautions:
Keep a good eye on your child. Make sure they are close by. Also check to see if the crowd is "getting to him" or is she bored looking at the sleeping lion?

Activity Story

Today I am going to the zoo.

I will see many animals. There may be many people there too.

Sometimes the animals or the people make noises. I will be okay because I will walk away if the noise is loud.

Sometimes the animals smell different. I may think they smell bad. It's okay because I can walk away from those animals.

When I walk away or walk around the zoo I will walk with a friend or my family.

If I am hungry or need the bathroom I will tell my friend or family. I know where to go because I think about my map. My map tells where places are at the zoo.

If I get tired I can tell my friend or family. We can sit and rest.

After we have seen the animals we will go back to the car. It will be time to go home (back to school).

1. Going to the zoo 
2. Looking at the animals from the map 
3. I can ask to go to the bathroom 
4. Eating at the zoo 
5. Leaving the zoo 
6. Exit

THE ZOO (Review)

Why Are We Doing This?
To review the experience of going to the zoo.

Materials:
Map made during preparation
Pictures of zoo animals
Plastic zoo animals

General Rule Of Thumb:
1. Pull out the map and pictures/objects you made in the preparation activity.
2. Have child move through the map and place the pictures/objects in the correct places on the map.
3. "Talk" about what you saw at the zoo. "What did you see first, second....last?"
4. Sing the songs about the zoo that you sang in preparation.

Do It Yourself:
Practice again the language you learned in preparation and at the zoo. Have the child place the pictures/objects where they should go.

And Furthermore:
Depending on how tired the child is, review when you get back or do it the next day. You can also pull out the map as a leisure activity, pretending to go to the zoo.

Activity Story

I went to the zoo and saw the animals.

I can tell my family (friends) about what I saw and did.

I will say "First, I went to the _____ and saw the _____. Next we saw the _____.

I will tell them my favorite animal was _____.

I ate _____ for lunch.

I can show them my map and show them where I walked.

My family (friends) will like to know about my trip to the zoo. It will make them feel happy to hear me tell them I had fun at the zoo.

I saw elephants

We walked here _____, and ate _____.

I love the zoo.

BOWLING (Get Ready)

Why Are We Doing This?
To prepare for bowling (the real thing). To anticipate the actual event.

Materials:
Picture schedule
Money

General Rule Of Thumb:
1. Develop a picture schedule of what you are going to be doing. (i.e. go on bus, get shoes, put shoes on, get ball, etc.)
2. f appropriate, have student get the correct amount of money for shoes and bowling. If necessary make a card to match coins. Also, you may need money for a snack if you will be buying it at the alley.
3. Review how you will get there. By bus, car, or walking?

Choices:
Let child decide which kind of snack they will buy at the bowling alley.

Do It Yourself:
Have your child put together his/her own schedule for the day.

And Furthermore:
For younger children you could have a play bowling set to practice on.

Cautions:
Try your best to prepare your child for all that will be happening; the noise, the waiting, etc.

Activity Story

I will go bowling on _____.

I will ride on the bus (or in the car) to get to the bowling place.

I will go bowling with my friends (or family). There will be other people at the bowling place.

I need money for bowling. I will put the money in my wallet.

I can think about what it will be like when I go bowling. I will need special shoes. I will wait my turn. I will roll my ball when it is my turn. It may be loud at the bowling place.

I will think about how fun bowling will be.

Go bowling on

I need shoes

Need money

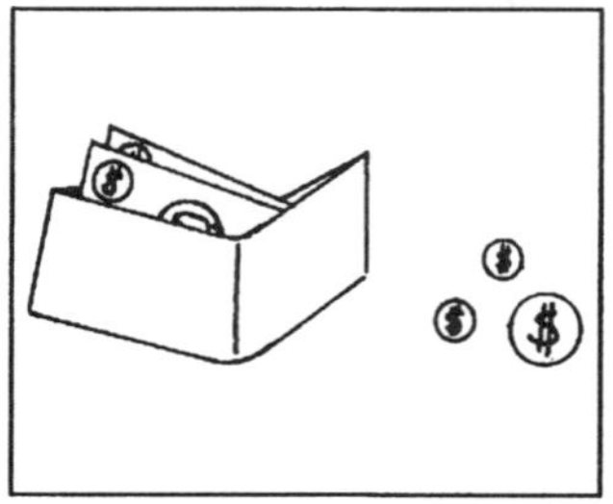

Roll my ball

I will ride the (car, bus)

BOWLING (The Real Thing)

Why Are We Doing This?
Fun of course. There is ample opportunity for language building and social interaction too!

Materials:
Money for admission and snacks

General Rule Of Thumb:
1. Review and practice rules of safety.
2. Standing in line to wait can be very difficult. Try to minimize the time but it can also be a good language time. "What are we waiting for?" "What do you see?"
3. Assist as necessary in requesting shoes and paying. Remember to encourage them to do it themselves as much as possible.
4. Assist with shoes and bowling skills.
5. How about a snack? May be a good time to practice interaction with others; requesting, choice making, money management.
6. Assist as necessary to remove and return shoes and say thank you.

Choices:
Depending on the ability or experience of the child, bowling can be kind of scary. Allow the child to choose as much as possible and yet encourage participation. They may need the choice of where to sit away from noise and still watch until their turn. Other choices may be which ball, which lane.

Do It Yourself:
Encourage independence, especially dressing skills. Practice asking for help, more, my turn, or I want a turn.

And Furthermore:
Bowling can be fun for children but this exercise can also be a language and social interaction time. Talk about what the child is doing, experiencing and/or seeing. Encourage teams or draw attention to others playing nearby. Some bowling alleys offer bumpers for the gutters. Ask to see if they're available.

Cautions:
Remember to be sensitive to the sensory intake of these children, some sounds may make their ears hurt at first.

Activity Story

Today I am going bowling. I remember, and think about our planning to go.

I will go in the car (bus) to get to the bowling place.

When I get to the bowling place, I will need to get special shoes. Sometimes I have to wait until people in front of me get their shoes. Sometimes I can get my shoes first. I will get in line.

I will change my shoes. Then I get my bowling ball.

[*Change if using the ball rolling adaptor.]
I sit and wait for my turn. When it is my turn I hold my ball up. I walk to the line and roll my ball down the lane.

I try to knock the pins. Sometimes I knock many down. Sometimes my ball goes in the gutter and I miss them all. When the ball hits the pins it makes a loud noise. That's okay. If I don't like it I can put my fingers in my ears.

That is okay. It's fun to try.

When the bowling is over I put my ball away. I change my shoes. I give the special ones back.

It's fun to go bowling. Sometimes I can go with my family. Sometimes I can go with friends.

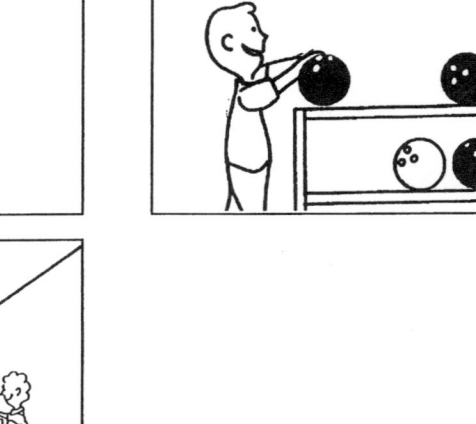

BOWLING (Review)

Why Are We Doing This?
To review the trip to the bowling alley and the game.

Materials:
Schedule

General Rule of Thumb:
1. Bring out the schedule you made. Talk about each thing you did. Good time to practice the new words you learned. ("Loud", "strike", etc.)
2. If you had a good time, schedule another time to go (what day next week would you like to go bowling?)

Choices:
Allow your child a choice if he/she wants to go bowling again.

Do It Yourself:
Let your child put his/her own schedule together (what did you do first? next?).

Activity Story

I will think about my trip bowling. I will tell my family (friends) about what I did.

I went to the bowling place with _____. I went in a _____.

When I got to the bowling place I got some special shoes. I put the shoes on.

I went and got a bowling ball.

I rolled the ball _____ times. I hit _____ pins. (My score was _____.)

It was loud when people hit the pins.

I liked bowling and think I might do it again.

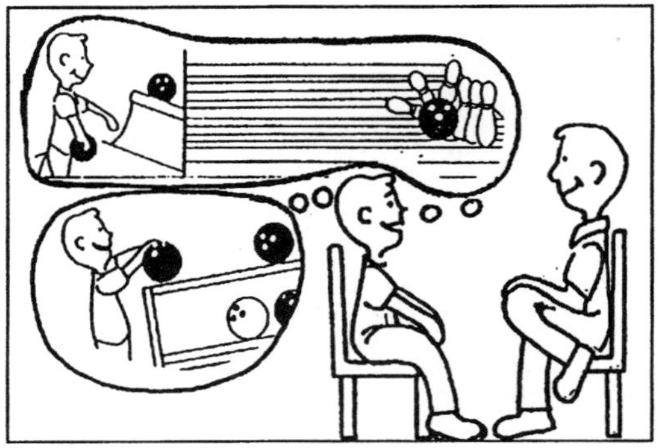

WHAT'S TO EAT? (Get ready)

Why Are We Doing This?
To plan and buy a "picnic" lunch or snack. Use with the food preparation card.

Materials:
Pictures of food cut from magazines &/or newspapers
Scissors
Glue

General Rule Of Thumb:

1. Plan the menu using the child's communication system.
2. Place the items vertically on the paper.
3. Make a shopping list of items you will need.
4. Check cupboards and mark what you have.
5. Look at a store advertisement. "Do you see any items we need?"
6. Review money needed. You may need to help estimate and/or trace amount on a piece of paper and let the child match shapes.
7. Let's go to the store.
8. Walk safety, enter quietly, pick out only the items on your list. Take items to check out, give money, and say thank you.

Choices:
Provide opportunities in child's communication mode to choose the kind of foods he/she wants.

Do It Yourself:
Encourage the child to manipulate and label the pictures of food items as much as possible. For children who do not understand pictures have them label actual objects. Have student find the pictured item on the shelf and place in shopping cart.

And Furthermore:
You can expand this task to include academic skills such as writing, math, ongoing food planning. Also preacademics such as cutting, pasting, and general skills of street crossing and greeting the clerk.

Cautions:
Safety is a must when crossing the streets!!

Activity Story

We are going (on a picnic, to the park). What shall we take to eat?

I can choose _____ (#) of food items.

I will make a list of what we need.

I will go to the store to buy my food. How much money will I take?

I will walk to the store safety. I will stay on the sidewalk and wait at the corner until no cars are there (or it says to walk) and then I will walk across the street.

I will find the food I want. I will put them in the cart. I will walk to the checkout stand. I will wait quietly.

When it is my turn I will give the cashier the money.

I will take my sack of food and walk safety to my house.

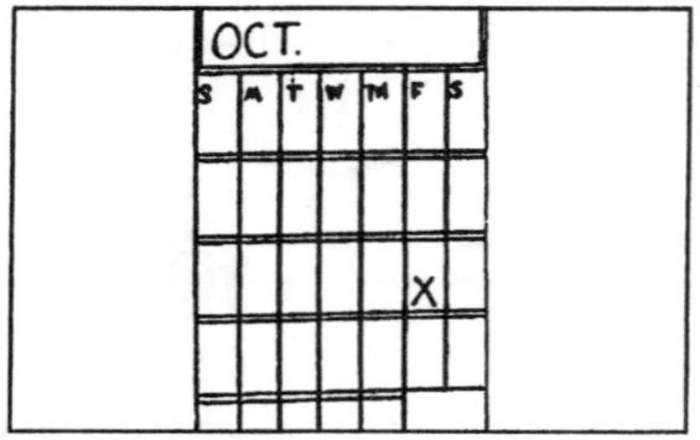

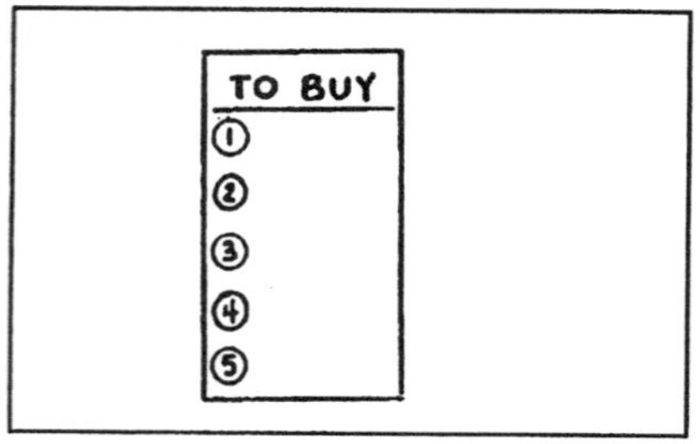

IN THE PARK (The Real Thing)

Why Are We Doing This?
To learn language through experiences of sight, sound, and motion. To experience physical exercise.

Materials:
Prepared picnic lunch
Markers for boundary if needed

General Rule Of Thumb:
1. Getting there safety comes first. Practice street crossing and other safety skills.
2. Walk the boundaries and give visual cues if needed. "Don't go past the flag!"
3. Take time to assist the child on each piece of equipment. Many times he/she will repeat the same action over and over. Try to encourage them to try new things.
4. The park is a great time for language building. Always comment on what the child sees or is doing. If the child is nonverbal you might say, "Are you looking at the yellow flower?" Motion is one of the best language experiences. Tell them while they are doing.

Choices:
After exploration of all the equipment give the child choices of activities. They can play by themselves but encourage changes and re-ask their choices sometimes.

Do It Yourself:
Up or down a scary slide or getting a swing to go are all good opportunities to get attention or ask for help.

And Furthermore:
If the child has difficulties with transitions be sure to give the child a concrete cue to when you are leaving. "You can go down the slide one more time and then it's time to go."

Cautions:
Be sure to keep an eye on your child, some children love to run!

Activity Story

We are at the park.

There are (swings, slide, climbers, tether ball) at the park.

I can (stay in the bark dust, on the grass, in front of the trees).

First, I will play on the _____.
Then I will play on _____.

I can ask for help if I need help.

I will try one new thing while at the park.

At The Park

Go to the park	Symbols will tell me where I can be.	Slide
Swing	Monkey bars	Finished

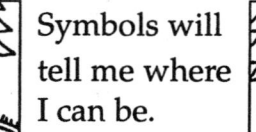

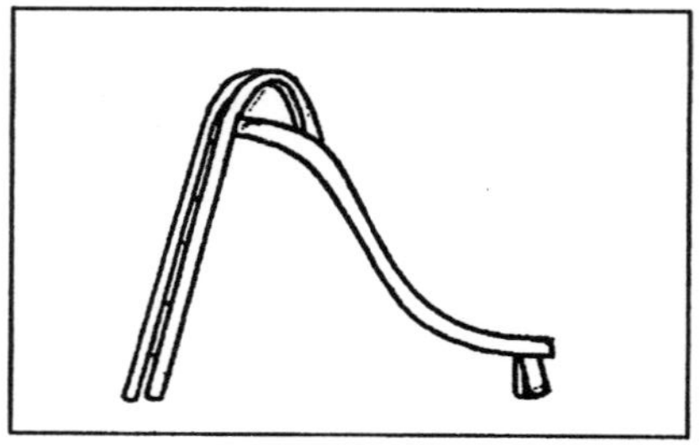

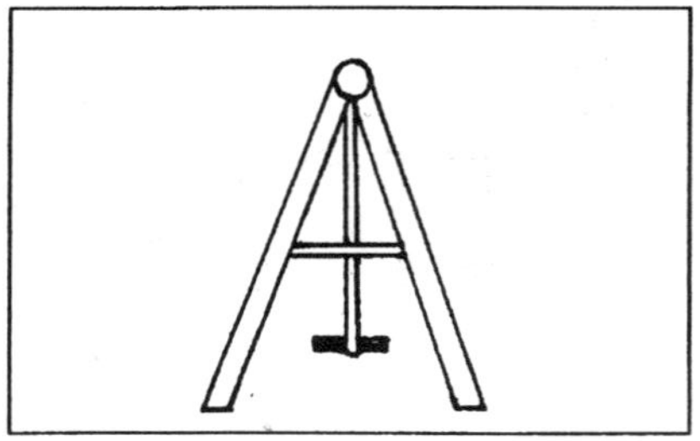

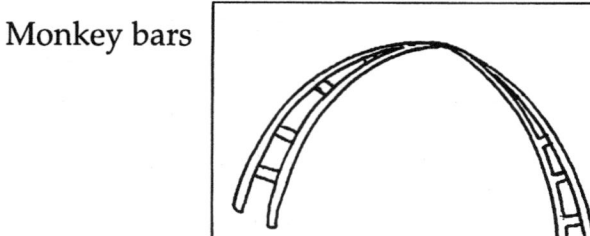

IN THE PARK (Review)

Why Are We Doing This?
To review the trip to the park and the equipment we went on.

Materials:
Visuals
Possibly pictures of the actual equipment played on.

General Rule of Thumb:
1. Show the schedule of the park or the pictures of the equipment.
2. "Talk" about what the child played on at the park. Introduce concepts such as first, second, third.
3. If appropriate, schedule another trip to the park.

Be sure that you are at the language level of the child.

Choices:
Allow choice of whether they want to go again and what equipment.

Do It Yourself:
Allow child to "review" schedule or look at pictures when he/she wants.

Activity Story

I will think about the fun I had at the park. I will tell my family (friends) what I did.

I went on the swings. I went up the ladder of the slide and went down the slide. I climbed on the bars.

I ran at the park. I stayed in the park.

When I need help I asked for help.

When it was time to go, I walked away from the park.

Visual Presentation here.

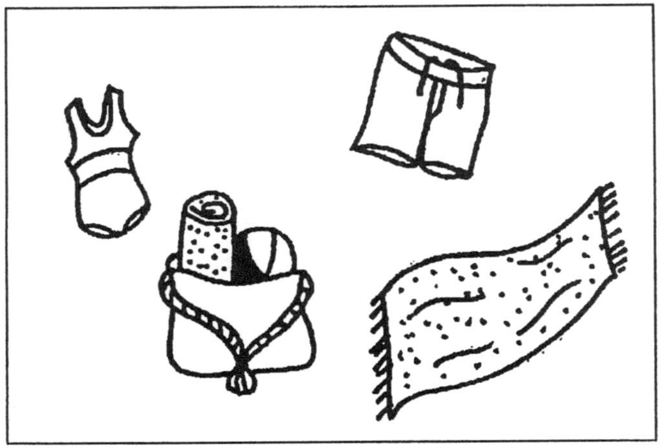

SWIMMING (Get Ready)

Why Are We Doing This?
To prepare to go swimming. To pack a bag with the necessary supplies.

Materials:
Bag for supplies
Bathing suit
Towel
Money

General Rule Of Thumb:
1. Depending on your child's ability, place swimming on the calendar. Will you go on Wed. p.m. or Fri. a.m.?
2. Using pictures, words, or objects review with your child what he/she will need.
3. Have your child pack his/her own bag using picture/word list.
4. Determine how much money you'll need. Depending on his/her ability have them match actual coin or coins to cans.
5. Discuss how you will get there. By car, bus, or walk?
6. On the way there review the rules of the pool. (i.e. no running)

Choices:
Let the student choose what swimsuit he/she wants to wear if they have more than one. They can also choose which towel they will take. "Do you want the blue one or the brown one?"

Cautions:
If your child has trouble with water, try water play first to get him/her used to the feel of water.

Activity Story

I will look at my calendar to see when I will go swimming.

I will go swimming on (after)_____.

I will look at my calendar to see what I need to take to the swimming pool. When it is time to will get my bag. I will put my swimsuit and towel in my bag.

I will take my (swim card, money) with me to get into the pool.

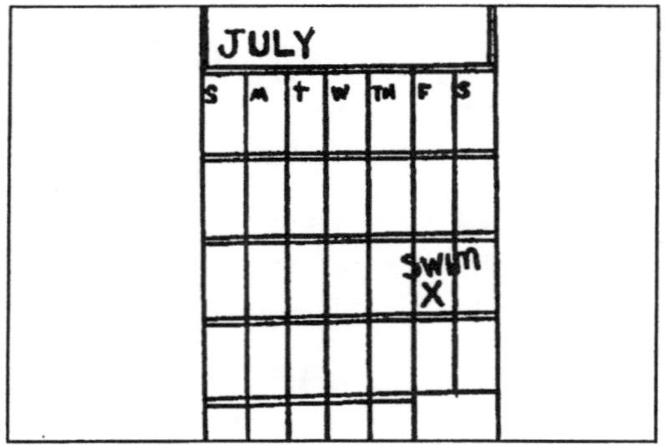

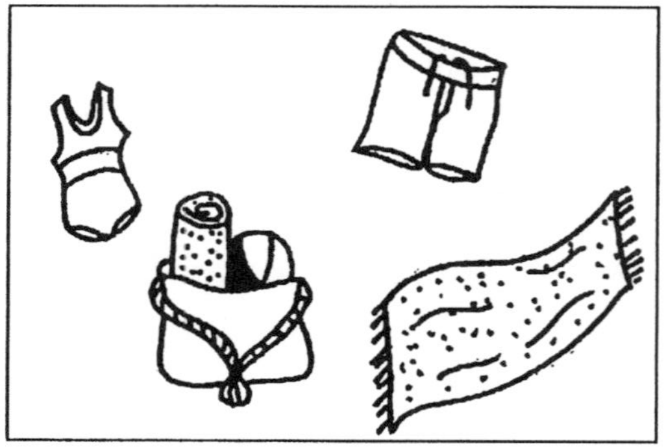

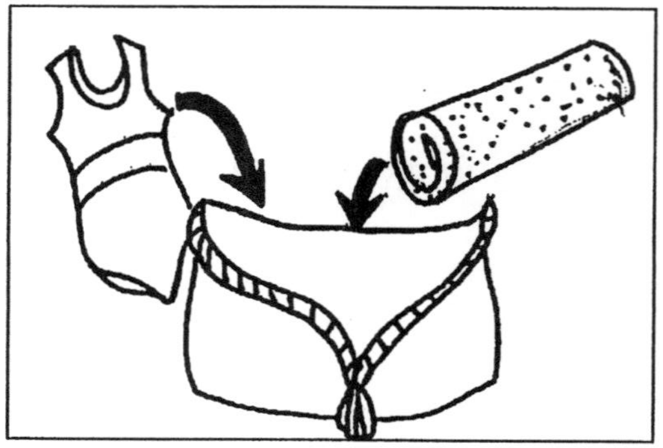

SWIMMING (The Real Thing)

Why Are We Doing This?
This is a sensory processing experience. It includes social interaction, language experiences, self help dressing skills, and most importantly FUN!

Materials:
Bag with prepacked swimming suit, towel
Money

General Rule Of Thumb:
1. Review the rules of arrival and safety.
2. Greet the staff with or without payment.
3. Assist as necessary with dressing to prepare for the pool.
4. Into the water....oh boy! Remember to label or comment on the children as they experience the movements (i.e. in the water, head under the water, jumping in).
5. Let the children know the end is coming. "Two more jumps and we'll be all done." Let them anticipate the end not find themselves out of the water.
6. Into the showers. Assist as necessary in dressing.

Choices:
In the water encourage the child to request what they will do or play with. For example will they use a kick board, a ball, or go off the diving board if they are an experienced swimmer.

Do It Yourself:
What a great time to practice dressing skills! But you may also need to practice asking for help. Remember to review "all done" or "finished" so the child learns an end will come and does come to fun activities. Let reluctant swimmers choose how much and how long they will be wet.

And Furthermore:
Swimming is usually either wonderful or terrible for these children. Some really enjoy the sensory experience. They are relaxed and are ready to experience motion and movement to be labeled and learned. Other children strongly resist the sensory feel of the water. Encourage them to get used to it.

Cautions:
To help prevent tantrums, remember to give them adequate warning to anticipate the end. Also, keep an eye on your child at all times, even the experienced swimmer!

Activity Story

I will walk into the swim area. I will give the cashier my (card, money).

I will walk into the locker room. I will take off all my clothes and then put on my swim suit. I will put my clothes into my bag. I will put my bag into a locker. I will ask for help if I need help.

I will take a shower before I walk to the pool.

I will walk to the pool. I will only jump in the pool where the life guard tells me I can.

I will swim/play in the water.

I will ask my friend to swim/play with me.

I will get out of the pool when I am asked and walk to the locker room.

I will take off my swim suit and put on my clothes.

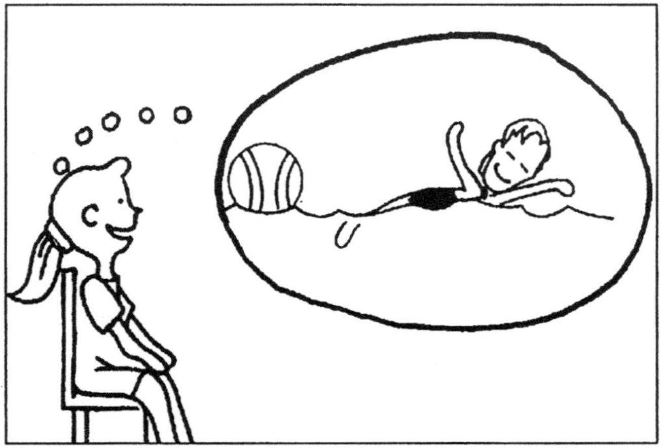

SWIMMING (Review)

Why Are We Doing This?
To review the experience of swimming.

Materials:
None

General Rule Of Thumb:

1. "Talk," using words and pictures, about swimming. "What did you do?" "What was your favorite activity?"
2. If you took photos or a video, use this to center your "talk" around. Label actions/activities.
3. If your child enjoyed this activity make plans to go again. "What day next week should we go swimming again?"

Choices:

If possible give your child a choice if he/she wants to go swimming again. If swimming was a struggle put some time in between swimming trips.

Activity Story

I went swimming on _____.

I had fun. I swam and played in the pool.

I will look at the pictures _____ took while I was at the pool.

When will I go swimming again? I will look at the calendar.

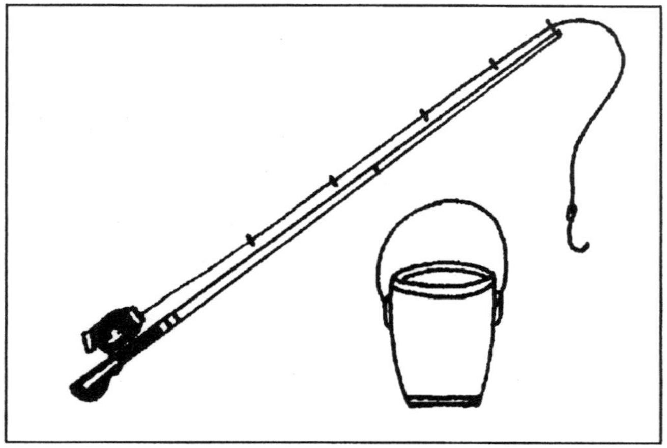

FISHING OH BOY (Getting Ready)

Why Are We Doing This?
Preparing for the many steps of going fishing to make sure it's as fun as possible.

Materials:
A story about fishing, sketches about it, the pole and even some bait if possible. If there is a choice, maps of where to go; if it's a set destination, then a map of it.

General Rule of Thumb:
1. Review the whole process in general, we go, bait, throw in catch, take off, keep or let go, clean up, come home.
2. Then review the details, the map of where you go, where to stand to fish, where the bait goes and where the fish bites, how it feels when the fish tugs, how you pull it in, where it goes or how to let it go, do you do more, when will you be done. Use the objects and pictures as much as possible.

Choices:
Where will you go? How many fish shall we try to catch? Shall we keep to eat or let go?

Do It Yourself:
After introducing the sequence of events review again but let the child try the baiting, throwing, etc. him/herself.

And Furthermore:
There may be stories in the library about fishing or fish.

Caution:
Watch the hook.

Activity Story

We are going fishing, oh boy. I will look at a map and decide where we are going.

Today I will practice how to put bait on the hook. Bait is food the fish like to eat. I put it on the hook so the fish will bite the hook. I will practice making the bait on the hook go in the water. I have to be careful when I swing the pole. I cannot let it touch anyone or any object.

It's fun to go fishing and fun to practice fishing too!

Let's get our stuff

I'll practice throwing the bait in

Where shall we go?

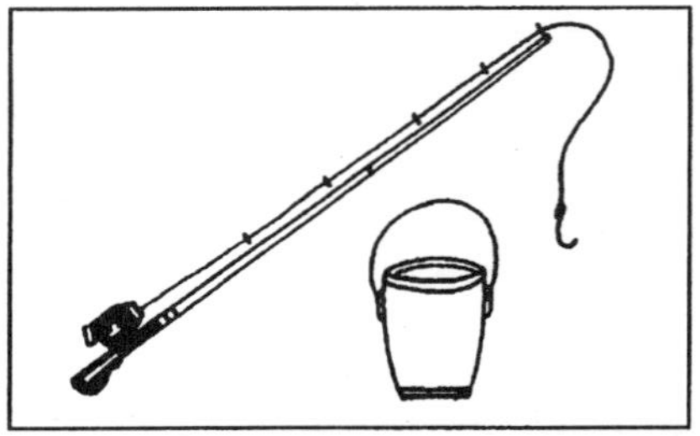

Let's practice getting bait on

I'm ready - let's go!

FISHING OH BOY (Real Thing)

Why Are We Doing This?
It's great to be outside!

Materials:
Fishing pole with hook
Bait
Holder for fish we catch
River, stream or farm

General Rule of Thumb:
1. Show your child the limits of space. At a farm give them a specific area to stand in. By a river or stream be sure to set how close to the water is okay to stand. How far up and down stream is okay to walk. Maybe use a stick as a marker or to draw lines.
2. Bait the hook and help them throw it in the water. Tug on the line to show them how it feels if a fish comes.
3. Explain they'll have to wait. Relax, enjoy, hang out!
4. If or when you catch a fish, help them remove it and re-bait - more?

Choices:
Do they want to bait? Do they want to pull in the line and check? Where do they want to "put in"?

Do It Yourself:
Encourage independence as much as possible but they may need support at some of the sensory issues. Bait, removing the slimy, flopping fish are all sensory issues.

And Furthermore:
Talk about what to do with the fish you catch. If you don't cook and eat it, then let them go.

Caution:
Hooks on fishing lines are tricky for anyone. Be careful to well supervise as the hook appears harmless, but it's not!

Activity Story

Today I am going fishing. I will go with my friend to a (farm/river). I will stand by the water. I will not get in the water. My friend will show me where to stand to be safe.

I will get bait on my hook. I will use my pole to swing the bait into the water.

Now I wait for a fish to swim by and eat the bait. Sometimes a fish comes by and eats the bait. Sometimes it takes a long time for a fish to come and eat the bait. Sometimes no fish come.

Waiting is difficult but I can look around me and see all kinds of pretty things.

If a fish eats the bait on my hook I will tug on the line. I will pull the fish in to the edge of the water. My friend will help me get the fish off the hook.

I can let the fish go back in the water or I can keep him to eat. The fish will flop and wiggle. Fish don't like to be out of the water.

If I catch a fish or if I don't, it will be time to go home. I can take my fish home or I can go home without a fish. It doesn't matter because I went fishing. It was fun.

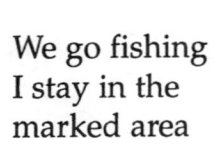

We go fishing I stay in the marked area

We put bait on the hook

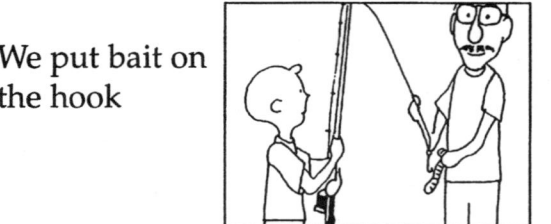

I throw the bait into the water

We wait for fish

If one bites we pull it in

You can let it go or keep it

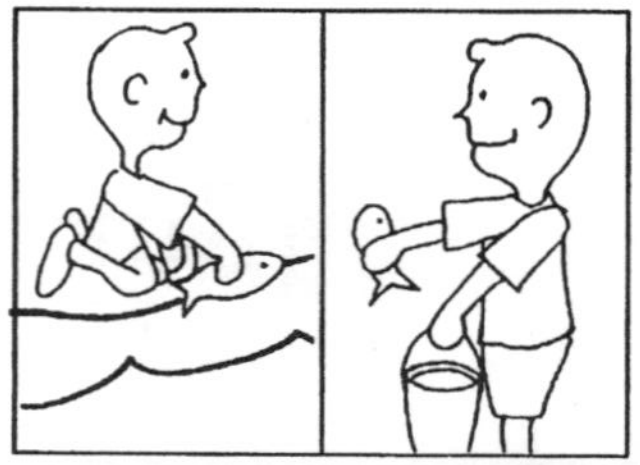

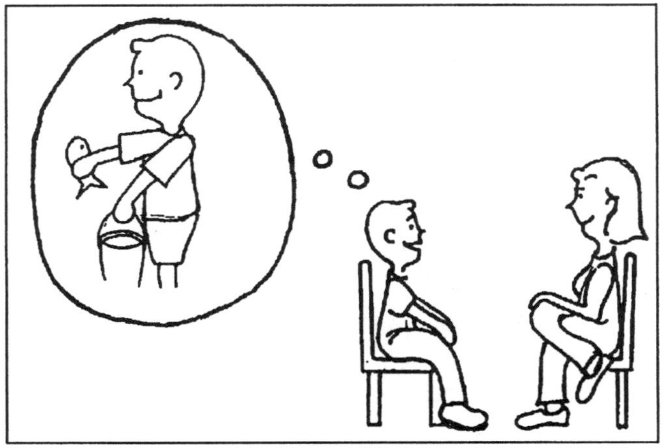

FISHING OH BOY (Review)

Why Are We Doing This?
To find out how well liked fishing is!

Materials:
The fish and pictures or sketches of the adventure.

General Rule of Thumb:
1. Sequence your pictures, sketches or words to talk about the day. What was the most fun? What wasn't?
2. What shall you do with the fish? Depending on your child, maybe you can talk about if you let it go, where did it go. Where do fish live? If you kept it, clean it and either have the child help cook it or cook it. Yum!

Choices:
Do you want to fish again?
How shall we cook it?

Do It Yourself:
As much as possible, encourage independent retelling. Either verbally or through pictures.

And Furthermore:
This could lead to a science lesson on fish or a cooking lesson too.

Caution:

Activity Story

I went fishing. I caught _____ fish. I went to a (farm, river) to fish. It was fun.

I went to the (farm/river) and stood carefully by the water. I did not get wet. I helped put bait on the hook. I threw the bait in the water by swinging the pole. I had to wait for a fish to come by. It was hard to wait but I did it!

A fish came by and took a bite of my bait. It made my line wiggle. I pulled my hook in. There was a fish. Oh Boy. It made my line wiggle. I pulled my hook in. It wiggled and flopped. That is okay. Fish wiggle and flop out of water.

My friend helped me take the fish off. It wiggled and flopped. That is okay. Fish wiggle and flop out of water.

We put it back in the water. It swam away.

or

We put the fish in our basket.

We put more bait on and fished again. When we were done we went home!

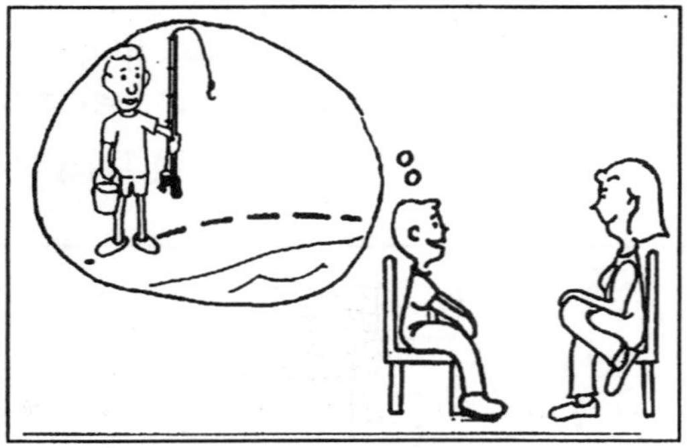

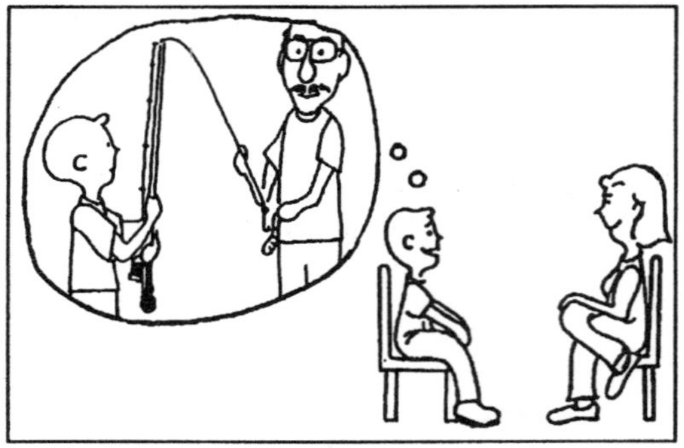

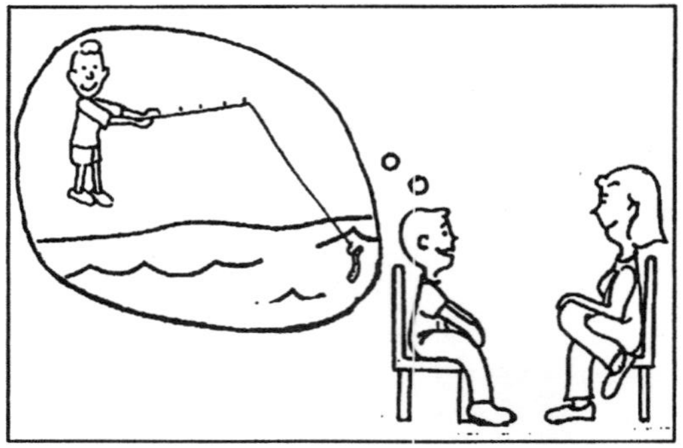

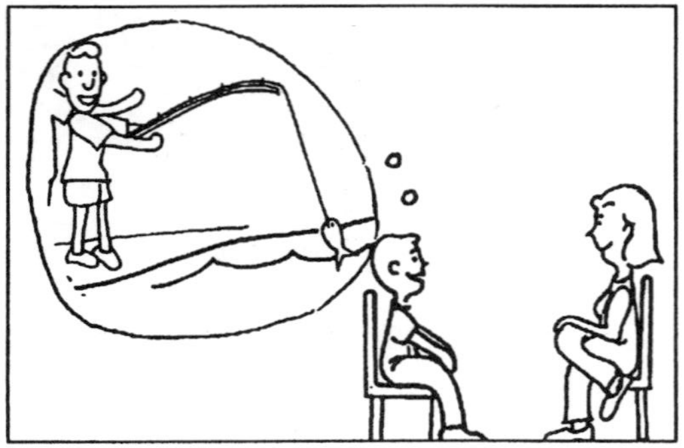

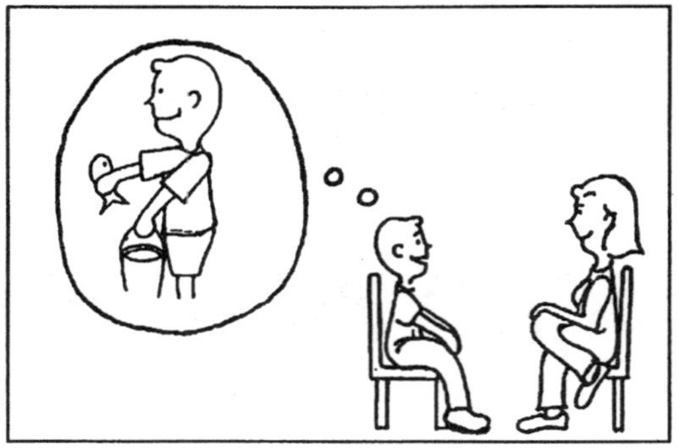

LET'S CALL A FRIEND

Why Are We Doing This?
To call friends on the phone and talk with them. The individual will need phone skills for this one!

Materials:
Pictures of friends
The friend's phone number
Pictures of activities the friends like

General Rule of Thumb:
1. Make a personal phone book by placing the friend's picture on a sheet of paper and the phone number on it.
2. Add pictures, sketches or words about what that friend likes.
3. Some individuals may need a script to follow. On your individual pages you may provide the basics of asking to speak to a friend and talking or asking to speak to a friend and they are not available!

Choices:
Lots to choose in your own phone book. Who goes in? Your friends and maybe the local pizza place?

And Furthermore:
Carefully prepare the individual for using the phone (see caution). If the child is interested but having trouble you may want their teacher to review or train phone skills. Remember this is a fun leisure activity not a lesson.

Caution:
Be sure to know how the individual uses the phone - NOT to call 911 unless it's an emergency and NOT to repeatedly call people for no reason.

Activity Story

Talking on the phone with my friends is fun. I pick up the phone and dial their number.

When I hear someone say "Hello" I will say "Hello, this is _____. May I please speak to _____." I will have to wait for that person to come to the phone. Sometimes it is a long wait - sometimes not very long. If my friend cannot come to the phone when I call, that's okay. I will call again another time.

When I talk to my friend, I will ask many questions. They may ask me questions. We will take turns asking the questions. Some questions I might ask are: "How are you today?" "What have you been doing?" "How is your family?" There are a lot of questions I can ask. If I forget or am not sure, I can ask my mom or dad for help.

It is important for me to know when it is time to stop. Sometimes we will have no more questions. Sometimes my friend may need to stop talking on the phone and go somewhere. When it is time to stop I will say, "Goodbye, it was nice talking to you." I will wait for them to say goodbye and hang up the phone.

It's fun to talk to friends.

Let's make a phone book.
Put pictures of your friends in

Put their numbers by their pictures

Write or put pictures of things they like or how we met to remember what to talk about

Call your friend!

Games
Activity Cards

MR. MOUTH

Why Are We Doing This?
To encourage turn taking in games, fine motor skills, and to have fun!

Materials:
Mr. Mouth Game, see "And furthermore" section on assembly.

General Rule of Thumb:
1. Assist as necessary to pass out chips to matching colored hand.
2. Adult, peer, or student turn on mouth section.
3. Assist as necessary to place chip on hand and flip.
4. Demonstrate or encourage child to get chip in the mouth.
5. Assist to know when finished and all chips are gone. See "And furthermore" section before beginning game!

Choices:
Present the choice of colored flipper hands. Then have them match the colored chips. Ask how many chips to use.

Do It Yourself:
Encourage independence in playing the game. This particular game has natural consequences. The mouth won't open to your chip unless you've waited the appropriate turn. Be ready to jump in with "help" if necessary before stress or frustration builds so that the game remains fun.

And Furthermore:
The flipping skill is sometimes difficult. It might be best to attach just one hand and practice awhile first. Leaving the head piece off helps practice too.

Cautions:
The fine motor skills required can be difficult for some kids. Assist the children as necessary and develop acceptable goals. Partial participation may be putting the chip in when it is their turn.

Activity Story

Mr. Mouth is a game you can play by yourself or with others.

There are round chips that are different colors. Each player gets to pick a color. Sometimes someone chooses a color I want. That's ok, I can choose another color.

There are round chips that different colors. Each player gets to pick a color. Sometimes someone chooses a color I want. That's ok, I can choose another color.

Someone turns the "head" on. The head goes around and the mouth opens and shuts.

I try to get the chips in the mouth by placing the same color chip on the same color hand. When the mouth is open I pull the hand down and lit go of the hand. The chip flips toward the mouth.

The game is finished when (all the chips have been flipped, one person gets all their chips in the mouth, or when all the chips are in the mouth).

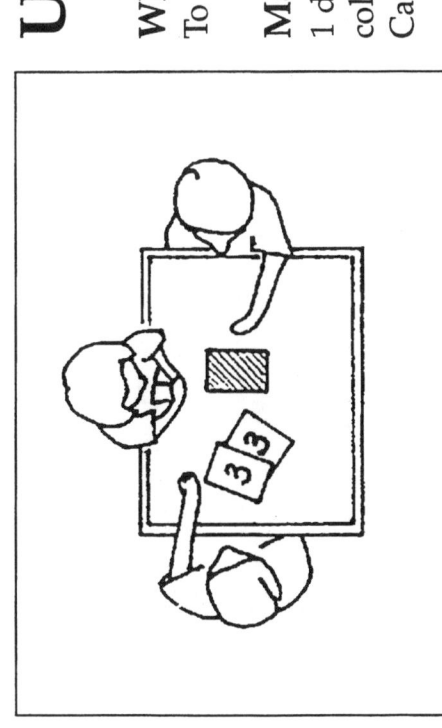

UNO CARDS

Why Are We Doing This?
To encourage dyadic interactions and have some fun!

Materials:
1 deck of Uno cards, sort if necessary to minimize color matching (i.e. 2 colors) and switching cards (i.e. only reverse cards) Card holder (optional)

General Rule of Thumb:
1. Assist student as necessary to either deal the cards or receive the cards.
2. Prompt as necessary to take the turn matching either color, number or other choice cards.
3. Prompt and assist as necessary to draw a card.
4. Help if necessary to identify when the game is "finished."
5. See "And Furthermore" for other adaptations.

Choices:
Practice the choices that are possible before playing the game. Show the child that either the color or the number can match. Explain the use of the reverse card etc. Keep the game simplified by limiting the type of cards used.

Do It Yourself:
Role play when it is your turn and my turn. If turn taking is difficult, reduce the number players or take the reverse and skip cards out.

And Furthermore:
The rules need to be clear and static. Uno is good only if it remains clear. Adapt each game for the individual child. Limit matching to colors or numbersonly if necessary. Remove any cards that may cause confusion.

Cautions:
Be careful when prompting for turns that you don't teach prompt dependence so that they wait to be told when to take their turn. Use different prompts such as verbal and tapping desk. Remember to WAIT for them!

Activity Story

Uno is a card game you play with friends.

I will get 7 cards. The cards will have numbers and colors on them.

One card is in the middle of the table. When it is your turn I take one card that matches the color or the number.

If none of my cards match, I pick one off the top of the extra cards stack.

I may see other cards too. A card that says draw four tells me to take four cards from the extra card stack. Draw two means pick up two. These cards do not have to match color or number.

I can play my cards with draw four or draw two any time.

I may have to draw 4 or 2 if the person before puts it down on the pile.

I may also see color cards with no number. They will say "S" or "R." An S means you must skip your turn. R means reverse and you go backwards.

If I put an "S" or "R" down, the color must match the pile.

If I put an S card down, the next person misses their turn. If the person before me puts down an "S" I miss my turn.

If I put an R card down the person who just had a turn opts to play again. If the person before me plays an "R," I will have to wait until everyone else has a turn before I can play.

When I have only one card left, I must yell "Uno" so everyone knows.

The game is over when someone has no cards left. I can have no cards and win. Sometimes, I will have cards when the game is over. That's okay, I may win next time.

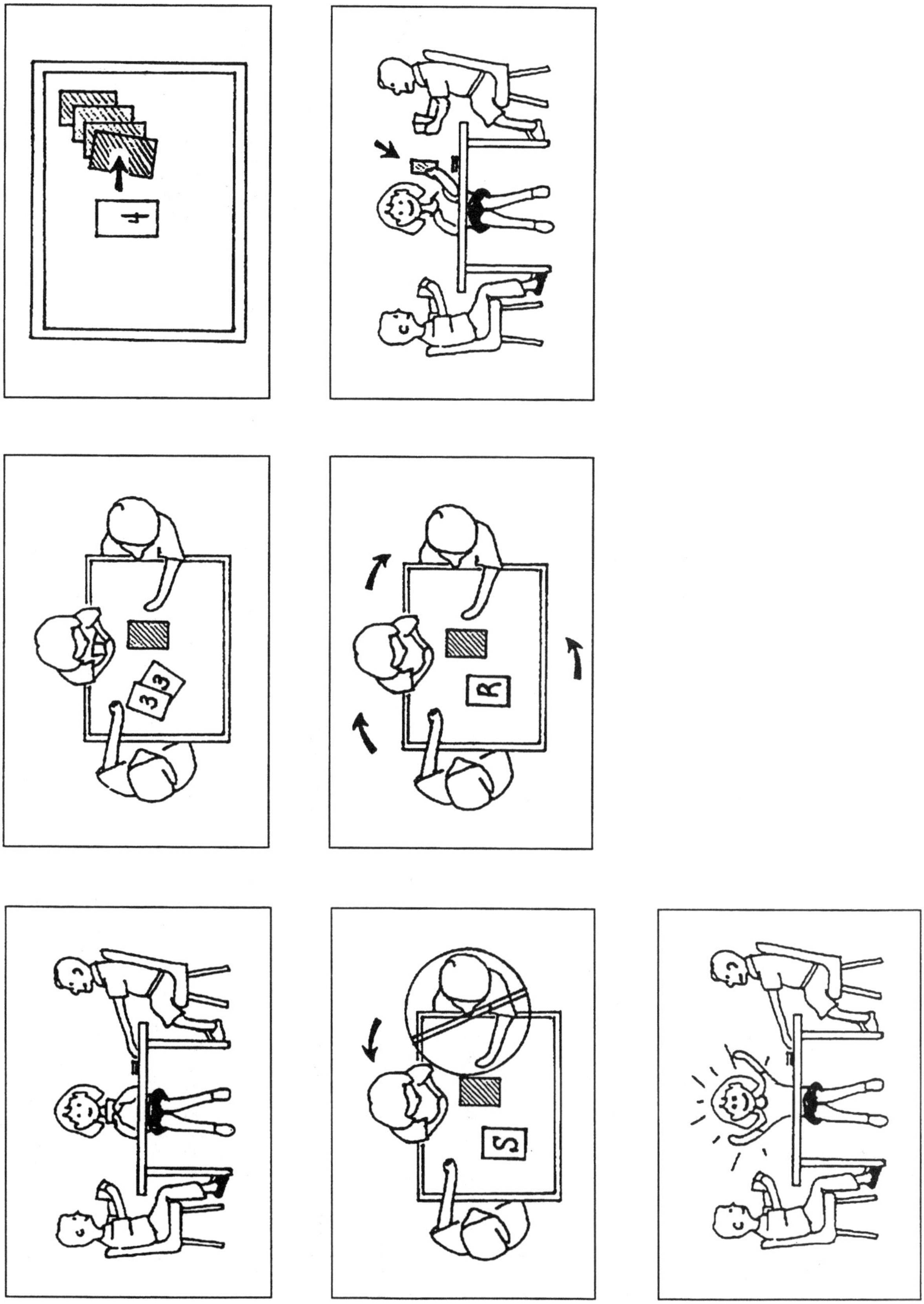

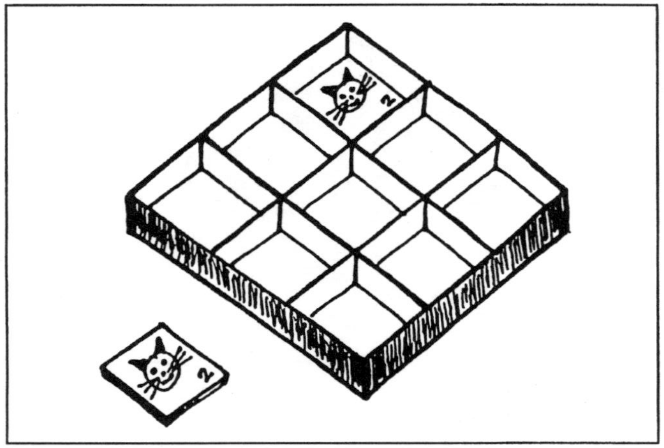

LOTTO

Why Are We Doing This?
To develop rote memory and fine motor skills. To learn a great leisure time activity.

Materials:
Lotto Grid
Set of lotto cards

General Rule of Thumb:
1. There are a variety of ways to play this game depending on the abilities of your child. Here are a few variations:
   A. Place a number of cards out face up (4 is a good starting number, add more if wanted or less if frustrating). Mix the matching cards up face down [?] and present to child. Assist in drawing one, turning it over and matching.
   B. Place 1/2 of the cards face down on the table and 1/2 in a stack face up. Take turns turning cards over until one is matched. Then go to the second card in the stack and continue.
   C. Put all of the cards face down. Take turns turning 2 over until a match is found.

Choices:
Present the cards used in the game. There are usually several sets of cards. Help the child decide which ones they will use this time. If possible, let the child choose how the game will be played this time. Encourage flexibility.

Do It Yourself:
Encourage independence, but offer help as needed. Let them ask for help if necessary.

And Furthermore:
Remember that games are easier with clear rules. The back and forth of turns is easier than introducing the idea of an extra turn with each match. Be careful that the game doesn't get confusing for some.

Cautions:
Encourage the child to learn turn taking, not prompt dependence. Remember to wait! Change from verbal reminders, to tapping the cards, to a motion, for prompts. These kids learn prompts as part of the game. Be careful what you teach!

Activity Story

Lotto is a game to play with friends.

First I place all the cards face down, so you can't see the picture on them. The cards fit into a grid which holds them.

Each person gets a turn.

When it is my turn, I turn two cards over and look at the pictures. If the pictures are the same, they match.

If two cards match, I will take them and keep them. I can then turn two more over.

If two cards do not match, the pictures are different. If the pictures are different, I will turn them back over so the pictures can't be seen.

When the cards don't match, my turn is over. I will need to wait until everyone else has a turn. Then it is my turn again.

I can watch and try to remember where the cards are when it is not my turn.

When all the cards have been matched, the game is over.

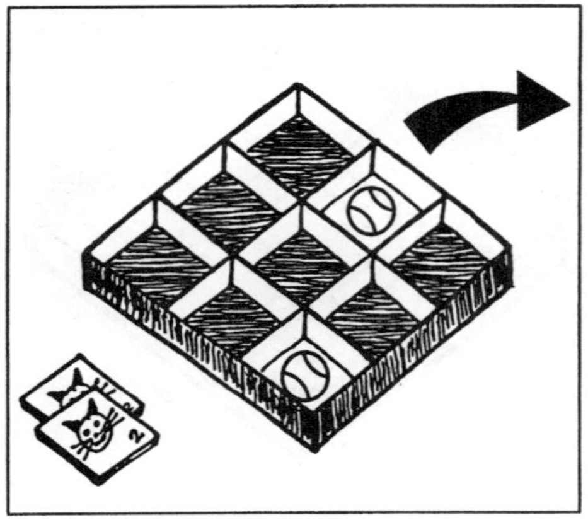

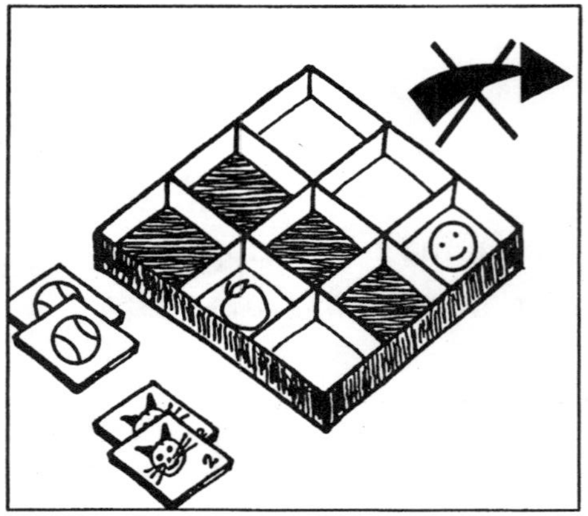

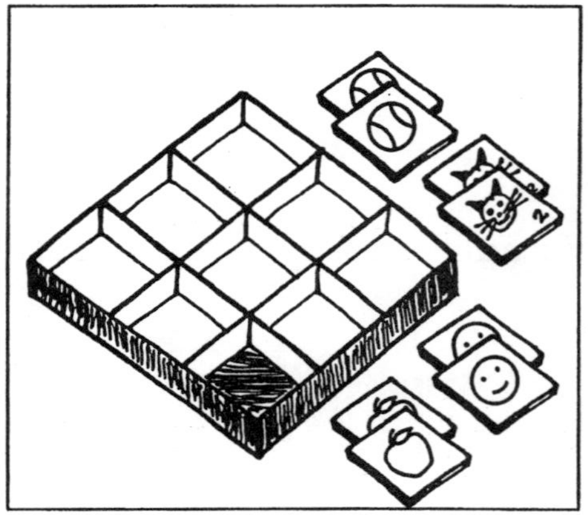

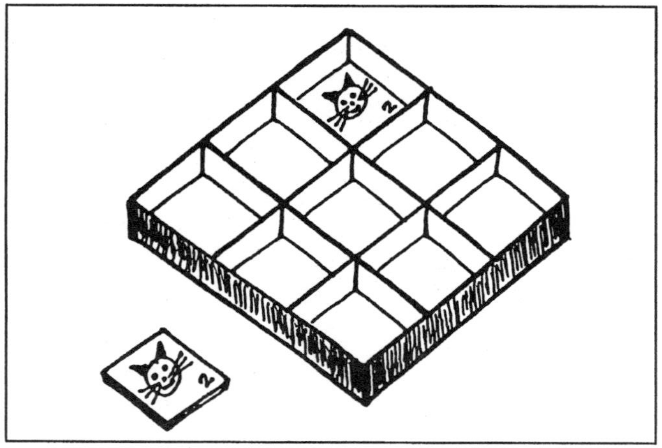

FAMILY AND FRIENDS LOTTO

Why Are We Doing This?
A fun card game with faces and places that are very familiar. Practice matching pictures and rote memory.

Materials:
A grid to hold pictures/cards; either from a real lotto game or paper with yarn glued on to form the shape of a grid. Duplicate pictures of family, friends, classmates, pets or favorite places and toys; cut pictures to uniform size and glue on a backing to make the pictures sturdier. You may want to coat with clear contact too.

General Rule of Thumb:
1. Place one set of picture cards in the grid, or have the individual place them.
2. If you know how many your students can handle great! Otherwise, experiment to find out how many cards to use at one time. For some students, one or two at a time to start is plenty.
3. Present the duplicate to the individual and encourage them to find x, or put with the picture of x.

Choices:
1. Have the individual choose which pictures to play with.
2. If they have a partner, they may choose who the partner matches.

Do It Yourself:
Encourage independence in all aspects such as retrieving the game, setting up, inviting a friend to play, playing (with many cards at a time) then cleaning up.

And Furthermore:
1. The first level of this game is simple matching. Other modifications could be:
   A. Turn the cards over and play regular memory.
   B. Make written word cards to teach intro to reading by matching a word card to the picture.
2. This is an opportunity to build language. Label the people (sign or words). Ask, wh- questions, "Where's mom," "Who's this?" Expand on comments and labels as much as possible.

Activity Story

Today I will play a game with a friend. The game has pictures I know because they are pictures of my family and favorite things.

First, I place all of the cards face down, so you can't see the picture on them. The cards fit into a grid that holds them.

Each person gets a turn. I can play by myself if I want.

When I'm taking turns and it is my turn, I turn two cards over and look at the pictures. If the pictures are the same, they match.

If two cards match, I will take them and keep them. I can then turn two more over.

If two cards do not match, the pictures are different. If the pictures are different, I will turn them back over so you can't see the pictures.

When the cards don't match, my turn is over. I will need to wait until everyone else has a turn. Then it is my turn again.

I can watch and try to remember where the cards are when it is not my turn.

When all of the cards have been matched, the game is over.

Visual Presentation here.

WAR CARD GAME

Why Are We Doing This?
To develop low level math skills and fine motor skills.

Materials:
Standard deck of cards with or without Kings, Queens, Jacks, Aces and Jokers, depending on the level of understanding.

General Rule of Thumb:
1. Separate the deck evenly by the number of people playing (two players is definitely easiest, but three could play).
2. Encourage the child to turn over the top card of their deck.
3. If turning the card over is difficult, start with the deck face up and the cards will be uncovered as the top one is removed.
4. Assist as necessary to determine who has the highest number. That person takes all the cards and puts them in a specified place.
5. Encourage the concept of "finished" being when the stacks in front of the player is gone. Check who has the most cards.

Choices:
There are really few choices to be made in this game except for, "Play some more?"

Do It Yourself:
Encourage independence in the turn taking. You can't determine who takes the cards unless everyone has turned their card up. WAIT! The natural consequences of waiting and taking turns is built into this game.

And Furthermore:
It may be overwhelming at first to use the whole deck. Try using a limited number of cards that will successfully hold their attention. Increase the number of cards used gradually.

Activity Story

War is a card game that you play with another person.

Each person gets the same number of cards.

When each person has their cards, they are stacked and placed face down.

Turn over one card. The person with the highest number card gets the two cards and they put them in a pile.

Now, turn over the next card. Who has the highest number? You do this until the game is finished. The game is finished when your stack of cards are gone, or when one person gets all the cards.

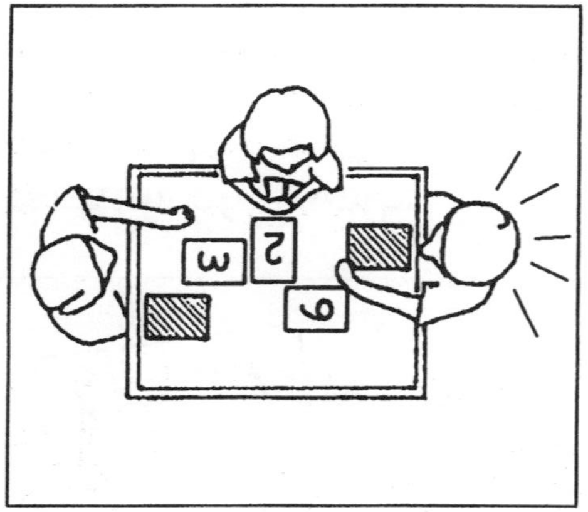

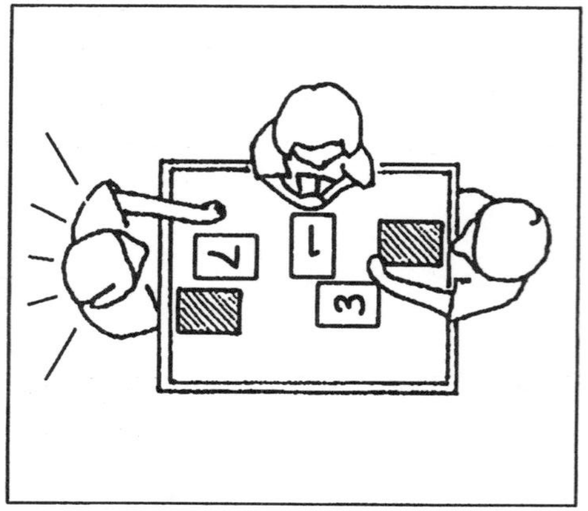

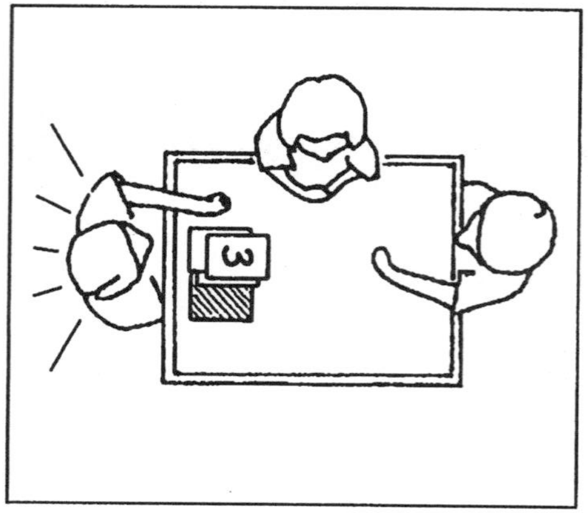

SORRY®

Why Are We Doing This?
Fun! Develop turn taking; increase math skills such as number identification, counting; and work on color recognition.

Materials:
Sorry® game

General Rule of Thumb:
1. Sorry has many rules. Be sure you know the rules before you present the game to your individual (see And Furthermore).
2. Set up the game allowing the players as much independence as possible.
3. If 4 markers make the game too long, try two markers.
4. Turn taking is a major goal in board games. Make it enjoyable (i.e. one other person playing, visual cue to indicate whose turn).
5. How will the game end? When the first person gets all the markers in home? When all players have their markers in home? Decide before the game and have as part of the game.

Choices:
Allow child to choose color of choice and who gets to go first; if he/she wants to play by him/herself or with others.

Do It Yourself:
Let the child pick cards, move markers. If difficulty with turn taking, develop a visual system cue to indicate whose turn.

And Furthermore:
Before playing, make sure you know the rules. Choose, depending on the child's skill level, the rules to follow - such as, will it be too frustrating to have to pick a 1 or 2 to get out of start or if you will use the "sorry" cards. Write the rules into your social story.

Cautions:
Start with 2 players only, so there will be little waiting.

Activity Story

Sorry is a game you can play by yourself or with others.

There are 4 different colored markers. I can choose the color I want to play with. I will place the same colored markers on the came colored start space.

I will turn over one card at a time. I will move my color marker the same number of spaces the number says to.

The person to get all their colored markers in the finish space is the winner. Let's see who is next.

Visual Presentation here.

CANDYLAND BINGO

Why Are We Doing This?
To build color matching as well as turn taking. To develop fine motor manipulation and have fun!

Materials:
Candy Land Bingo game
Spinner
Color dice
See tips in "And Furthermore" section

General Rule of Thumb:
1. After selecting a board, assist the child in placing men of each color nearby.
2. Assist as necessary to flip spinner or roll dice.
3. Assist as necessary to retrieve correct color of man and place on appropriate circle on the board.
4. Children with autism need clear starts and stops. Assist as necessary for successful turn taking, but also to clearly see the finish (fill whole board, use of number of men in their pile, put one of each color on).

Choices:
Allow the child to select their own board if possible. Let them decide who will go first and if they want to use the spinner or roll the dice.

Do It Yourself:
Assist as necessary for the child to feel successful in manipulating the pieces. It may be necessary to help them understand a turn in this game. Remember to be visual and clear. Hand the spinner/dice to each player.

And Furthermore:
The whole card can be too much confusion for some children. Try covering some of the rows if it is a problem. All the cards have one row with one of each color in it. You may need to cover the whole card except for this row until the skills are learned.

Cautions:
Remember to encourage language development. Describe what the child is doing as he/she does it. "You're putting the blue shape on the blue circle."

Activity Story

Candy Land bingo is a game I play with my friends. I can play with one, two or three friends.

There are four different colors of men. There is one board with many different colored dots on it. There is a spinner with an arrow that points to one of the colors.

When it is my turn I will flick the spinner to make it go around. When the spinner stops I will see what color it is pointing at. I find a marker that matches that color and put it on the board, on a circle that matches that color.

I will wait for my friends to use the spinner, pick a marker and match it on the board. When it is my turn they hand me the spinner. When my turn is over I hand them the spinner.

We play the game until someone wins. Someone wins when they have markers on matching colors that go straight up, down or across like one side of an X.

Sometimes I might win, sometimes a friend will win. It's fun to play with friends even if I don't always win.

Sports
Activity Cards

HOPPING A-LONG

Why are we doing this?
To develop large motor and motor planning skills. It can be practiced alone or with a friend!

Materials:
Hop scotch pattern
Lucky charm/marker
Child who can hop from cue or prompt
Red stop sign (optional)

General Rule of Thumb:
1. Model and assist child to hop on one and both feet to complete the pattern as given in hop scotch.
2. Model and assist the child to hop around or over a square with the marker in it.
3. Assist child as necessary to place marker in the increasing squares of the pattern. You may need to assist in placing the marker in each square progressively.
4. When the marker has been in each square all the way up, or all the way up and back, the game is finished.

Choices:
Choices may be built in if the child wants to choose which square gets the marker.

Do it Yourself:
As much as possible encourage independence, but fun is the main goal. Allow the child to ask for help or assist them to ask if it looks like they need it. Helping a child to balance may make it more fun and after a few times they may be able to do it on their own.

And Furthermore:
It is up for grabs if the rules of old should stick. With some children you may be okay to say if they put their other foot down they are out. Others may need to just finish the pattern and an occasional foot down to catch themselves is acceptable.

Cautions:
Watch that the marker is not thrown inappropriately!

Activity Story

Hopscotch is a game I can play by myself or with friends.

I will hop on one foot or both feet. The pattern of squares on the ground tells me. If there is one square I use one foot. If there are two squares I use two feet.

I take a marker and put it in a square. I can not put my foot in a square with a marker. Each turn I put the marker in the next square.

A turn is when I hop down the pattern not putting my foot in the square with a marker. I turn around and hop back.

When I hop back to the beginning, I stop and pick up my marker.

Sometimes it is hard to pick up the marker. If I am on one foot, I cannot put my other foot down. It is hard to balance.

It is okay if I stumble or fall. I can do better next time.

When I play with friends, I must wait turns. It is my turn, up and back, then they will hop up and back.

A game is over when the marker has been in each square for 1 turn.

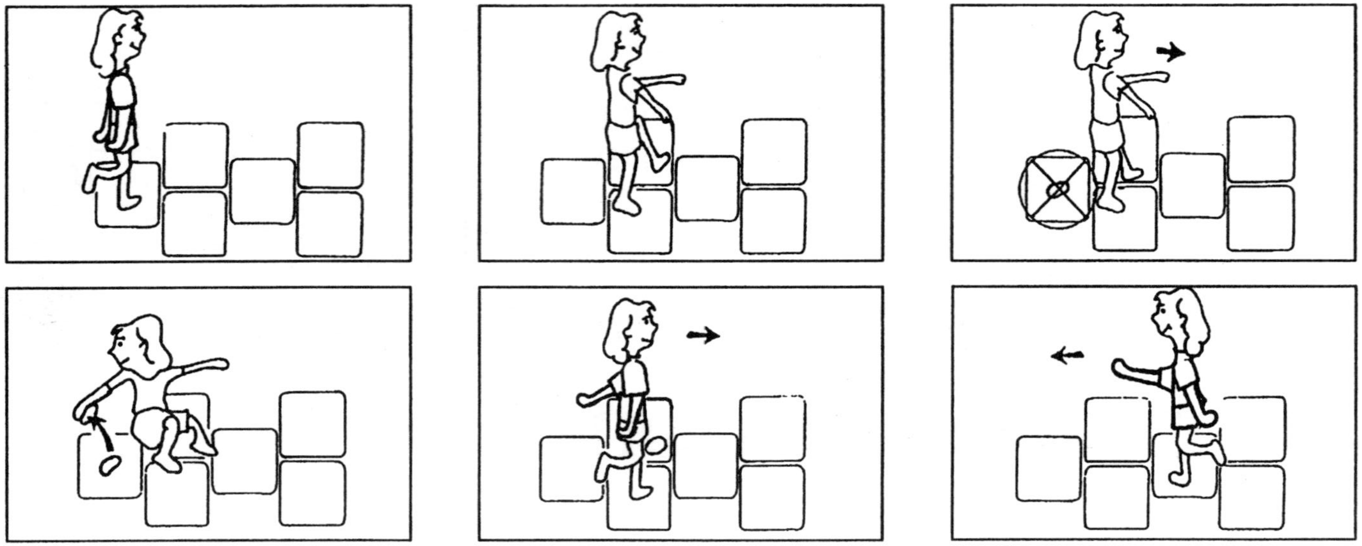

OBSTACLE COURSE

Why are we doing this?
Let's run and play! To learn sequencing actions and playing with friends.

Materials:
A variety of actions are possible besides those listed. However, think concrete or something with an object. Read "General Rule of Thumb" for more explanation:
Cardboard box with holes or other bean bag toss target
Socks filled with pinto beans (and knotted!!) or purchased bean bags
Paint sticks or chips and a coffee can
Old ties
Playground balls
Min tramp, sit and spin maybe a swing

General:
1. Set up your course with the concrete symbols. Start with the trampoline or sit and spin. While jumping, spinning or swinging, count off the time by dropping a paint stick into the can - (5 is a good number). When the sticks are gone, they need to grab the bean bag to have it right next to the trampoline. Once you have the bean bag, it's off to the toss. Once tossed, have the ball next to the box and you're off to the ball roll. Have the ties set up to indicate where to roll, bounce etc. Tape on the floor or string works well too! Then back to wait another turn.

Choices:
Not too many except they may choose to design the course.

Do it Yourself:
Try not to jump in with assistance too soon. The close placement of objects should be natural cues as much as possible.

And Furthermore:
There are a lot of ways to work on sequencing. Some individuals may need only two for a start. Others may need to wait in chairs lined up or carpet squares to see turn taking. Be creative with the activities, but think concrete.

Activity Story

Today I will do an obstacle course with my friends. An obstacle course is when I do different fun things one after the other. I may throw, kick, jump or run. I might even crawl through a tunnel. It's a fun game.

Today I will first jump on a trampoline until I hear it is time to move on.

I will grab the bean bag next to the trampoline and run to the throwing place. I will throw the bean bag at the target.

Next, I will take the ball next to the bean bag toss and run to the lines on the floor. I will roll the ball down the lines on the floor.

I will run back to my seat and wait my turn. My turn to do the obstacle course is when all my friends have done it too.

Sometimes the game may change. I may throw the bean bag first, or I will throw not roll the ball. The teacher will help me know what to do.

Let's play!

ON THE LINE

Why are we doing this?
A fun game to play outside with friends. It's a lot like tag or relay races and a good way to practice running games with friends.

Materials:
Bean bags per child
2 lines @ 50 feet away
2 papers with an x on them
2 groups of child in separate lines.

General Rule of Thumb:
1. It is critical in this game to explain the whole process or you'll have a lot of random running.
2. Using visuals and modeling demonstrate running with a bean bag; running to the other line and put the bean bag on the "x". You may want the person dropping the bag to yell "go" to indicate when the next person should start running.
3. Explain, use visuals, that everyone runs to the other end then the game is over. If possible, explain the team to get their bean bags all on the X first is the winner. (Remember that winning is pretty abstract and not the point of turn taking).

Choices:
Be creative. Choices maybe teams or bean bag. See ideas in furthermore for other ways to build choices.

Do it Yourself:
Try to be very clear about the game. Then step back and encourage the child to learn from the pattern of what is happening.

And Furthermore:
Substitute hopping, skipping or one leg jumps for the running. Try different things with the bean bag... on the head?

Activity Story

The game "on the line" is a game to play with friends.

There will be two lines of friends. I will stand behind a friend to wait my turn. I will hold my bean bag in my hand.

A turn means I run as fast as I can to the paper with the "x." I drop the bean bag on the paper.

I will know it is my turn when I see my friend in front of me drop their bean bag on the paper. They will yell "go" and I will run with my bean bag.

Sometimes I will hop to the paper. Sometimes I may skip. The teacher will tell us what to do.

Which ever I am told, hop, skip, or run, I will do as fast as I can. My friends will be happy if we do it the fastest.

ON THE LINE 2

Why are we doing this?
This game is an expanded version that requires handing off an item or a more complex pattern. Try On the Line 1 for a simpler running game.

Materials:
2 lines @ 50 feet apart
2 papers with an X on them
2 groups of children in lines
2 bean bags

General Rule of Thumb:
1. This game can be modified in many ways. You can always try different methods. However, try to include at least 1 handoff of the bean bag and a complete round trip: back and forth.
2. Demonstrate with visuals and modeling the entire game before starting. Then practice with the student with autism.
3. Assist as necessary but try to use visuals and gestures. Physical assist is very distracting during this type of game.
4. Explain again with visuals if possible that the game is over when everyone has had a turn. You may try to explain winning but the concept is very abstract and taking turns with your team much more important.

Choices:
There aren't too many choices here except teams. See And Furthermore for some other ways to play.

Do it Yourself:
Encourage independence, but also peer interaction. Let peers help guide them if they need it. They're part of a "team" after all and that means team work.

And Furthermore:
Substitute hopping or skipping as a way to expand or modify. Try the beanbag on your head or between your elbows.

Activity Story

The game "On The Line 2" is a game to play with friends.

There will be two lines of friends. I will stand behind a friend to wait my turn.

Sometimes a turn means to run to the paper and bring it back to the next friend. I give it to the person who stood behind me.

Sometimes a turn means I take the bean bag from the person in front of me. I run as fast as I can and drop it on the paper. I run as fast as I can back to tell the next person waiting to "go."

I can tell which turn because I will have a bean bag if I must run and drop it. If my friend says go and I don't have a bean bag, I must run and get it.

The game is over when everyone has had a turn to run.

My friends will be very happy if I go very fast when it is my turn.

BASKETBALL (SHOOTING HOOPS)

Why are we doing this?
Fun! Exercise. This is an activity that can be an individual activity, a parallel play skill or an interactive activity.

Materials:
Basketball hoop (there are adjustable ones)
Basketball - there are different sizes of balls for different sizes of children

General:
1. Decide where you will shoot hoops. At the park, at the school or in the neighborhood?
2. When teaching the skill, decide whether just one person will shoot at a time or more than one.
3. If the child does not have the strength to shoot at a full sized hoop, try to find a shorter one. (Elementary schools usually have shorter ones.)
4. Shooting hoops is for fun. Encourage participation and trying his/her best.
5. Shooting hoops does not have a clear end, so decide how you will indicate finished.

Choices:
Allow individual to choose to play alone or with a friend.

Do it Yourself:
Encourage independence. Remember to work on asking for help if he/she needs it.

And Furthermore:
This is a great activity for those individuals who like to throw. Encourage throwing only at the hoop. If individual has difficulty knowing what the hoop is, try "highlighting" the back board.

Cautions:
Watch for flying balls. Balls can come off the rim pretty fast. Also, if playing by a street, teach safe ball retrieval.

Activity Story

I will play basketball by shooting hoops.

Shooting hoops means to try to throw the basketball into the hoop. The hoop is the round rim with a net on it.

I can shoot hoops by myself or with a friend.

I need to watch the ball because it can come off the hoop and hit me.

I get excited when the basketball goes through the hoop. If the ball does not go through the hoop, that's OK. I can try again.

Shooting hoops is fun.

ROLLER SKATING

Why are we doing this?
Fun, Exercise

Materials:
Skates (traditional or rollerblades)
Protective wear (helmet; knee, wrist and elbow pads)
Money (if going to a rink)

General:
1. From the beginning have the individual with autism wear the protective wear. If it's an expectation from the start, it will be a lot easier to get them to wear them.
2. Be sure the individual knows the boundaries of where he/she can skate (if at the rink, what direction to go; in the neighborhood, how far can he/she go? From one corner to the next on the sidewalk.)
3. Practice! Practice with the person. If your individual is facility defensive and won't hold your hand, use a dowel that both of you can hold onto. Most rinks have a practice place. At home, walking in the grass gets people used to being on skates.
4. Have fun!

Choices:
Have the individual with autism choose when and where to skate when possible.

Do it Yourself:
Encourage independence as soon as possible.

Cautions:
If crowds or people close to them or noise overwhelm the individual with autism, limit rollerskating to the neighborhood. If you want them to get used to a rink, ask the rink if there is a "slow" time and schedule your time then.

Activity Story

It's time to go rollerskating.

I will put on my knee pads, elbow pads, wrist pads and helmet. Then I will put my rollerskates on. I will ask for help if I need help.

I will rollerskate in one direction at the rink.

I will rollerskate to the end, then back.

Sometimes I will fall down. That's OK. It will hurt sometimes and sometimes it won't. When I fall I can ask for help to get back up or I can get up by myself.

When it is time to stop, I will take my skates off and put them away. I will take all my pads off and put them away.

That was fun! I want to skate again another day.

Hobbies / Crafts
Activity Cards

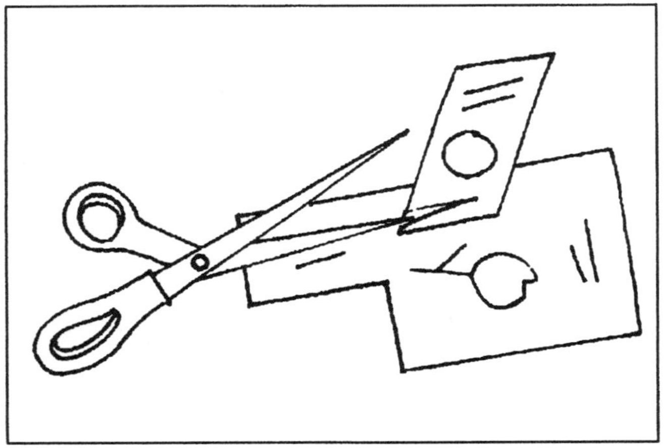

WHERE DOES IT GO??

Why Are We Doing This?
To learn how things are grouped and enjoy pictures of your favorite things!

Materials:
Catalogs, Colored Advertisements or Brochures especially:
   Toy Stores
   Grocery Stores
   Pet Stores

Firm paper such as poster board
Glue
Small boxes or baskets to hold cards

General Rule of Thumb:

1. Have the poster board precut into card size shapes (2.5 x 3.5).
2. If possible, have the individual cut out their favorite pictures from the catalogs. Mark with a black felt pen the line to follow. Assist as necessary.
3. Glue the pictures on the cards assisting as necessary. (You may want to cover with clear contact - see And Furthermore).
4. Set up the boxes or baskets with a sample of the different categories you've selected. Depending on the student you may start them with a sample in the basket, let them set up the samples or have the word of the category to match the picture to, i.e. "food."

Choices:
Have the individual choose their favorite pictures and categories. Remember some individuals have unique interests so let them build one of their own categories such as shoes!

Do It Yourself:
Remember this can be ongoing, do a few a session. Have collections to sort. Maybe they would like to look and stack sometimes too.

And Furthermore:
Oh boy, lots of cards - now what? How about a game of "Go Fish?" Deal some of the cards and have the individual request and make category matches. Or pick from the partner's hand if they can't ask and lay down matches as they come!

Caution:
As always WATCH THOSE SCISSORS

Activity Story

I like sorting pictures and thinking about where they go. Sometimes it is hard work and confusing but I can ask for help if I need to.

I will make cards by cutting out pictures from magazines or the paper. The pictures will be of things I like to eat, play with or wear. I will use glue to put them on cards. Then I am ready to play.

First, I look at the picture to see what it is. Can I eat it? Do I play with it or do I wear it? I will put all the pictures of things I can eat together. I will put all the things I play with together. I will put all the things I wear together.

When I am done I can mix them all up and do it again. I can cut more pictures out and add to the many pictures I have. Working with the pictures is fun.

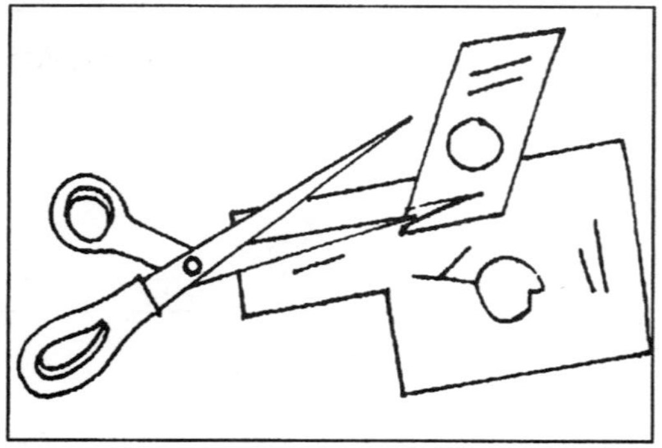

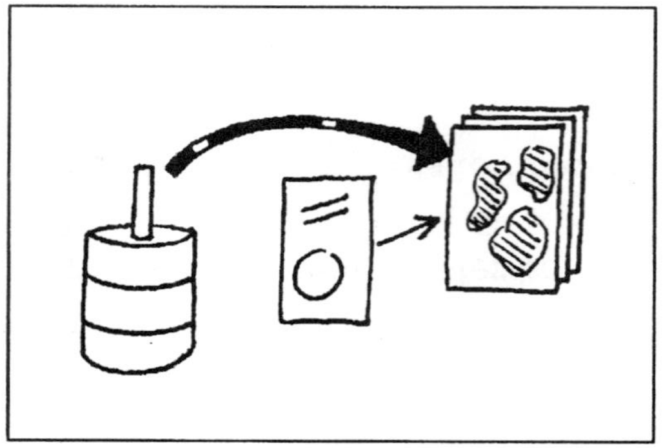

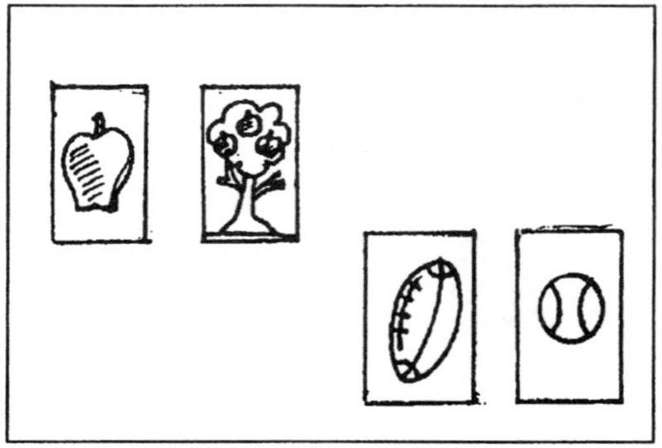

EGG HEAD

Why Are We Doing This?
To grow some sprouts to add to a salad or sandwich. Watching things grow is fun!

Materials:
Egg cup*
Paper
Permanent pens
Cotton balls
Water (spray bottle)
Bean or alfalfa sprouts

General Rule of Thumb:
1. The egg cups which hold eggs come in different styles and colors. Craft stores have paint if you need to make them plain white.
2. Have the child plan the face to put on the cup on paper first. Surprised, happy, sad, funny. Discuss the parts of the face and how to make it look happy, surprised, etc.
3. Once you've decided on a face assist as necessary to draw it on the side of the cup.
4. Assist the child as necessary to place the cotton balls in the cup and sprinkle the seeds on top.
5. Assist the child as necessary to water the cotton balls until moist (not drowned).
6. Mark it on the calendar to water it again tomorrow.

Choices:
Picking different faces is a good way to discuss emotions.

Do It Yourself:
Ideally having a finished, grown seeds cup to show would help the child know what the project is. Taking responsibility to keep it watered is also very important.

And Furthermore:
The egg cup holders come in different sizes and shapes. Try a variety for a diverse group. Alfalfa or bean sprouts grow quickly and easily. They're edible too if you want!

Cautions:
Watch those permanent ink pens. You need them so the face doesn't wash off when watering.

Activity Story

Today I am planting some seeds in an egg cup*. Seeds take time to grow and need water every day.

I will first decide on what kind of face to draw. It could be happy, surprised, sad.

After I have drawn the face on paper I will have to draw it on the side of the egg cup. I must be careful because the pen does not wash off. I may not get it on anything but drawing my picture.

I put cotton balls in the cup. I take a few seeds and put them on top of the cotton balls.

I will take the water sprayer and spray the cotton balls until they are wet. I will be careful to not spray a lot of water. I will not get anything but the cotton balls wet.

I will mark on my calendar to water my seeds everyday. Soon I will see the seeds sprout.

When the sprouts are tall I can eat them. They taste good in a sandwich! I will not eat the cotton balls!

*When they grow it will look like hair growing out the top of a head. It is a pretend head to watch seeds grow.

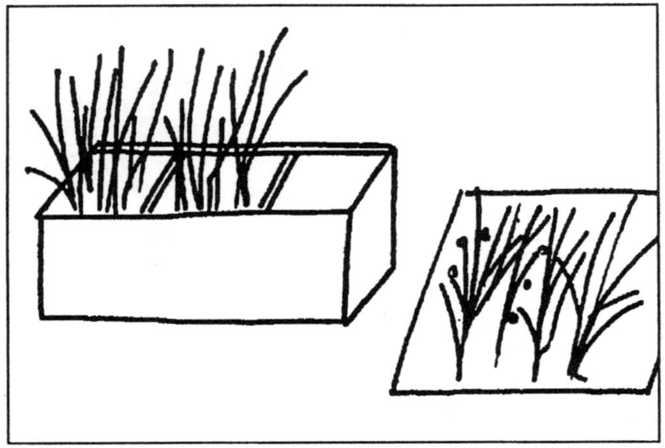

GROWING PLANTS

Why Are We Doing This?
.........Growing plants is fun! To watch the seeds sprout and grow to plants, then be able to use the plants in cooking.

Materials:
Container of prepackaged windowsill herbs or box or basket small enough to fit on a windowsill
Dirt
Herb seeds
Water in a spray bottle
Trowel

General Rule of Thumb:
1. Herb gardens are available in prepackaged containers. Open the package and use the following information as a guideline.
2. Set out the equipment you will need and label each item.
3. Assist as needed to put the dirt in the container and put the seeds in the dirt as each package directs.
4. Assist as needed to lightly water.
5. Show your friend a calendar and mark the days to water as well as when the plants should be ready.
6. Assist as necessary to collect the herbs by plucking or cutting (some may need to be left in a warm place to dry).
7. Package the herbs and share with family or friends.

Choices:
Different herbs are used for different purposes. Help choose some fun ones like catnip, or good smelling ones like mint.

Do It Yourself:
Once the seeds are planted the watering could be totally independent with a watering chart.

And Furthermore:
Herbs can continue growing so this could be ongoing. Maybe starting a garden could be a gift to mom itself.

Activity Story

Today I will start growing an herb garden. I will plant the seeds to grow.

I will take a container and fill it with dirt. I will put the seeds into the dirt.

I will water the seeds with the spray bottle. I may not spray water anywhere but on the dirt. I will stop when the dirt is a dark color.

On my calendar I will put down when to water the herbs and when they should be grown. I will water my herbs when the calendar tells me.

When the herbs look like the picture on the package I will pick or cut them.

Sometimes herbs need to dry. I will put them on a paper towel for 2 days.

After 2 days I will put them in a little plastic bag. I will write the name of the herb on a piece of paper and put that in the bag too. If I need help my friend can write it for me.

I can give my bags of herbs to family or friends. They will enjoy using them to cook with.

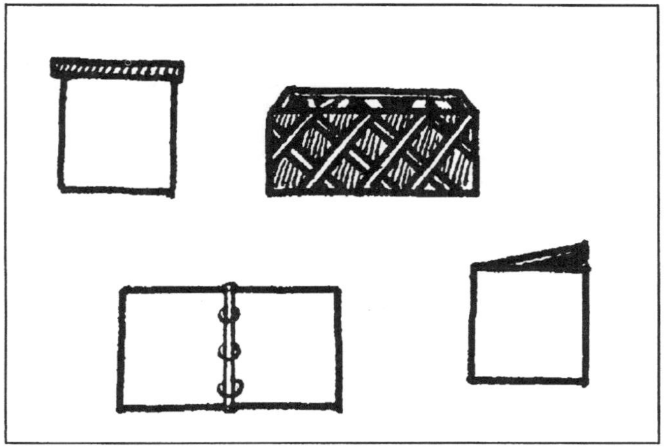

SCRAPPY TIMES

Why Are We Doing This?
To build on the interests of individuals. To create something to share with others.

Materials:
Adhesive backed album pages with plastic covers
Scissors
Old magazines, books, and newspapers, catalogues to order from

General Rule of Thumb:
1. Many children have strong interests in one particular area. It might be fans, dinosaurs or light bulbs. Discover what your child likes to look at or know about.
2. Assist as necessary to cut pictures related to the topic chosen or collect miniatures.
3. Encourage child to write or type something about the pictures they cut out.
4. Arrange the items on the pages of the album. See sections on back for more ideas.

Choices:
Allow many choices in this area. Let them choose what they want to put in their scrap book. Even samples of items are okay if they can fit. Try not to judge their interest but encourage expansion. If they like fans look at all the different kinds of fans.

Do It Yourself:
Encourage the chile do label by writing, typing, or dictating to you. Have them describe what the item is or what it means to them. Encourage the use of language!

And Furthermore:
Let this be an ongoing project. Maybe work on one page at a time and date the pages. Their interests may change and it will be fun to look back at what they used to like.

Cautions:
You may need to cut the items yourself. Remember to watch out for those scissors and kids who little sense of danger!

Activity Story

Sometimes people collect items that are very important to them. I like _____.

I like to look at my _____ so I will keep them in a special place. It could be boxes, a book or a notebook made especially for _____.

I will tell my friend what I want to collect. I will tell them what I want to collect _____ in.

My friend and I will pick a time to work on my collection. Sometimes it will be many times. Sometimes we won't have time. I know I will be able to work on my collection and that feels good.

1. Decide on an item to collect

2. Decide in what you will collect your items.

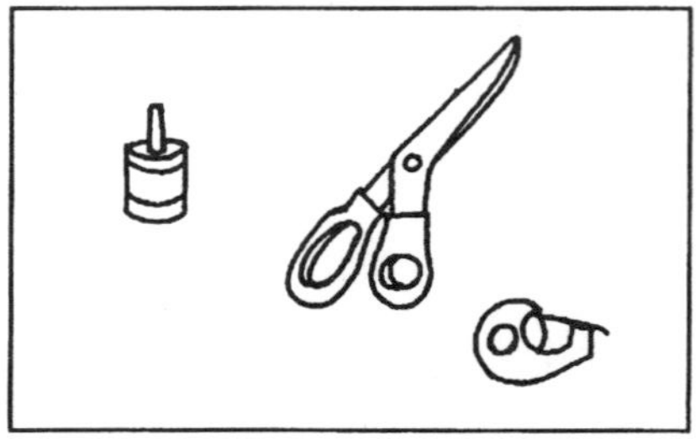

3. Gather your materials.

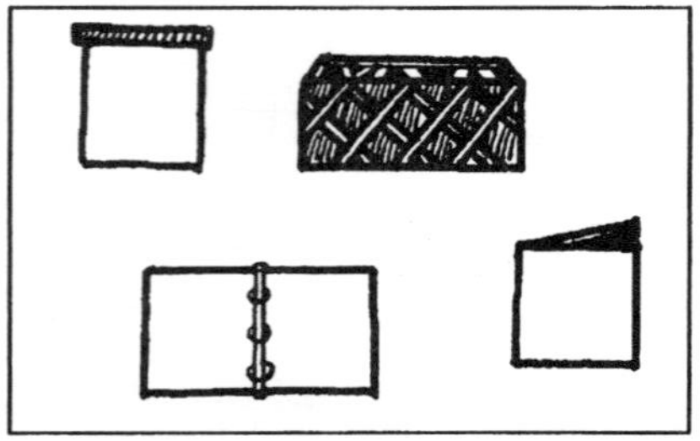

4. Work with your friend to make your scrap book.

5. Now you have a scrap book all your own.

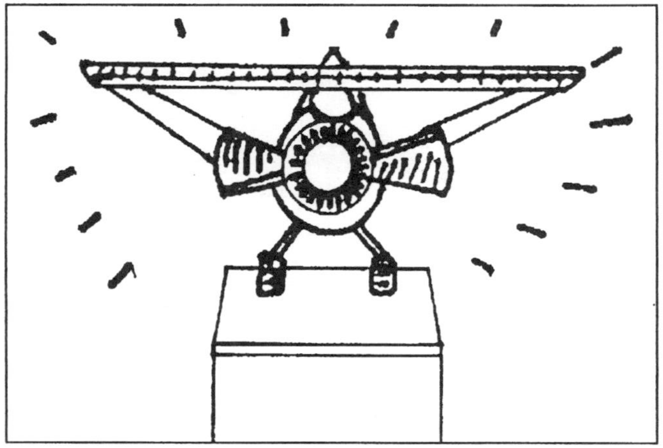

MODELING AWAY

Why Are We Doing This?
To build visual replicas that are interesting and fun. This can be a short term project or ongoing task.

Materials:
Model kit:
- car
- boat
- plane
- dinosaurs
- battery powered

Model glue

General Rule of Thumb:
1. Review the "whole" of it. Look at the picture of the finished model. Talk through the parts that make a whole.
2. Assist the child in laying out the pieces in sequential order of assembly.
3. Set clear expectations, especially if more than one day will be required. "Today we will make the frame, tomorrow we will put on the wheels, etc."
4. Do something with the finished model. Celebrate by showing it off or playing with it.

Choices:
Picking the model is a BIG choice. Then add the colors and other details needed to complete it. Sometimes the choice may be, "Do you want to do it yourself or do you want some help?"

Do It Yourself:
Encourage the child to ask for help as they need it. Try to move to independence with older or more able children. Step back and let them work! Let them ask for help if they need it. A great skill in a busy household!

And Furthermore:
Manipulating the necessary tools and pieces can be more difficult for some children. You may need to have some parts preassembled so it's not too frustrating.

Cautions:
Be careful to use good judgement in selecting a model that is appropriate for your child. Check the size and number of pieces. These children break, drop and lose pieces easily. This can be frustrating for them. Try to find a model with large, sturdy pieces. Also, keep your eye on the glue and tools!

Activity Story

A model is something you put together to make a _____ that looks like a real _____ but small.

This model makes a _____.

There are many pieces to the model. Each piece goes with other pieces. The instructions will tell which piece goes with or where.

We will glue pieces together. It's starting to look like a _____.

We may not finish it today, but we will do more tomorrow.

Model

Pieces

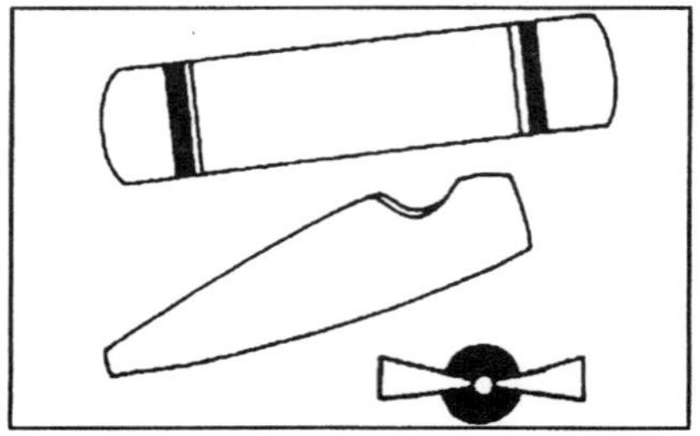

Glue

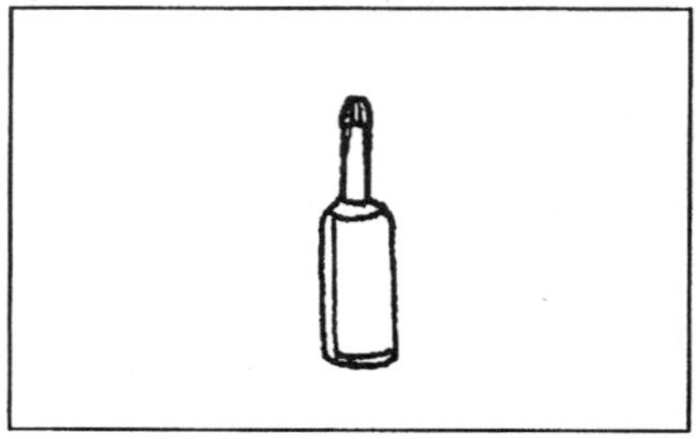

Put together

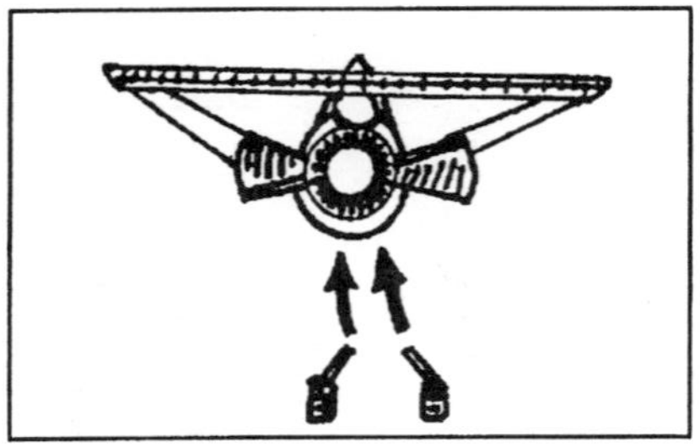

Let dry

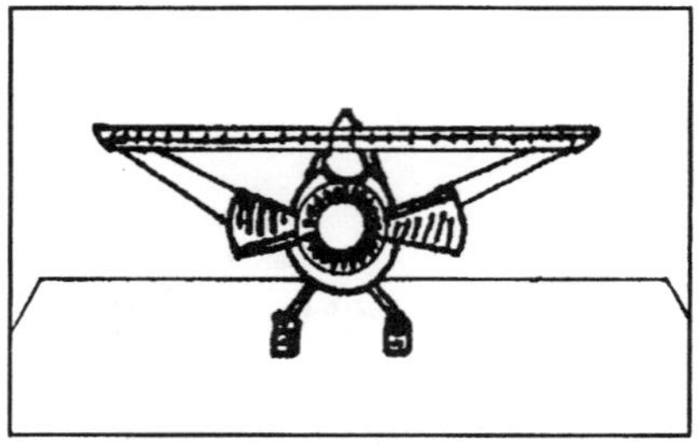

Finished

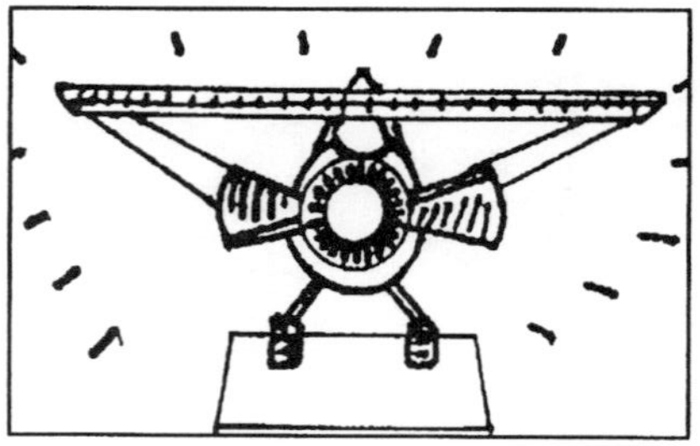

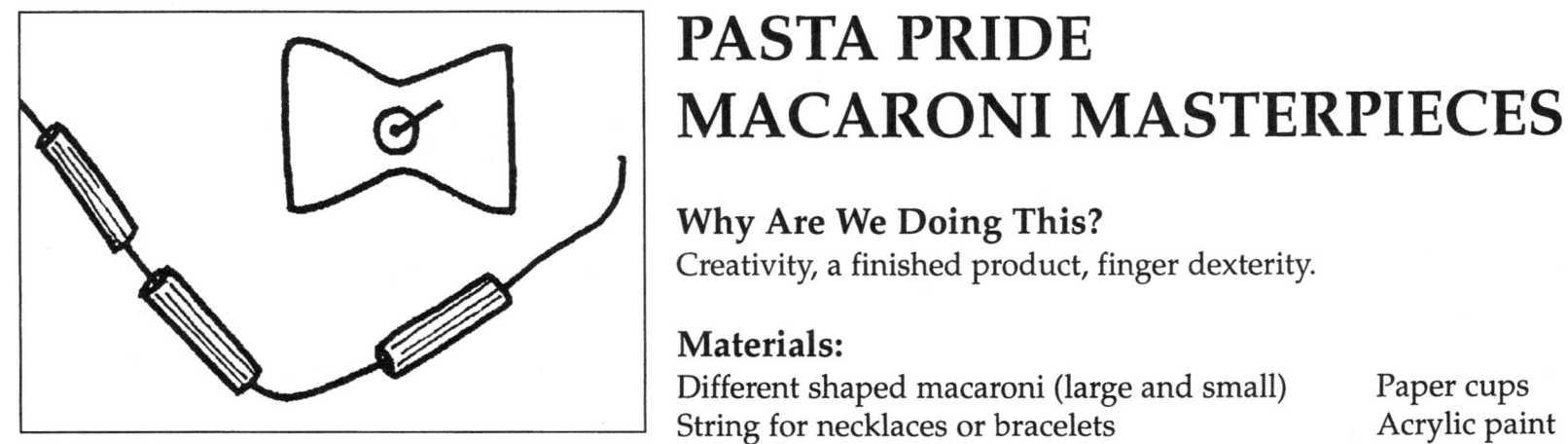

PASTA PRIDE
MACARONI MASTERPIECES

Why Are We Doing This?
Creativity, a finished product, finger dexterity.

Materials:
Different shaped macaroni (large and small)
String for necklaces or bracelets
Pin or earring backs
Metal barrettes
Magnets
Food coloring
Paper cups
Acrylic paint
Clear acrylic spray
Craft glue
Scissors

General Rule of Thumb:
1. Choose, or allow the individual with autism what he/she wants to make. Then choose what shape of macaroni to use.
2. If you want to color the macaroni, put drops of food color into water and then soak the macaroni for up to 30 minutes.
3. To dry the macaroni, place on waxed paper. Turn over every 15 to 30 minutes. To dry faster, place in a microwave on lowest setting for 2-3 minutes, turning every 30 seconds.
4. Spray with clear acrylic spray.
5. For necklace, string the hollow pasta or tie around solid pasta (such as bow ties). For barrette, pin or earrings, glue pasta on with craft glue. Or for a magnet, cut out a shape from thick paper or cardboard. Paint if desired. Glue pasta onto paper.
6. Allow the individual with autism to enjoy his/her masterpiece!

Choices:
Lots of choices available - shape, color, kind. Don't overwhelm with all choices - as much choice as is capable.

Do It Yourself:
Encourage independence. Let their creative juices flow.

Cautions:
Watch for eating especially after sprayed. If the individual with autism likes to munch on dry pasta, either give them a set amount that they can eat or make edible masterpieces.

Activity Story

I will make a _____. I will use macaroni to decorate.

First, I will place the macaroni into water that is colored. I can choose the color(s) to use.

I will place the macaroni on waxed paper and let it dry. I will wait until the timer to touch the macaroni.

The macaroni will be sprayed with acrylic spray.

I will put string through macaroni to make a necklace.

I will glue macaroni on barrette, earring backs, paper to make barrette, earrings or magnets.

What fun I will have making different things out of macaroni.

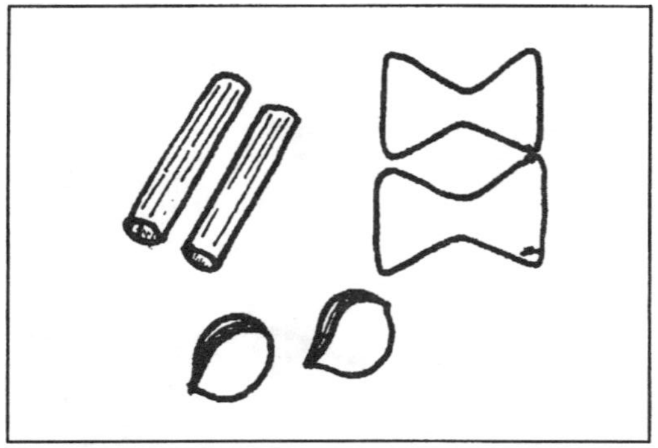

EARRING MAKING / FRIENDLY PLASTIC

Why Are We Doing This?
Creativity; sense of accomplishment; color/shape identification.

Materials:
Friendly plastic (you can buy it at craft stores)
Scissors
Earring backs
Craft glue (such as oven, oven mitts, foil, cookie sheet)

General Rule of Thumb:
Have the individual with autism retrieve the materials. Have in one spot and/or develop visual system to gather materials.

Set out in left to right sequence in the order of steps.

Allow as many choices as possible (see choices).

Remember, safety is essential - both with scissors and/or oven.

Assist, as necessary, in any of the steps.

Remember, its the individual with autism's creativity. Do not impress your "tastes."

Choices:
Let child choose what color(s) or shape(s).

Do It Yourself:
According to skill level, allow child to cut the friendly plastic, take cookie sheet in or out of oven, glue the backs on.

Cautions:
Ovens can be hot, scissors sharp!

And Furthermore:
Be careful when you place the friendly plastic in the oven because the plastic can move around.

Rule:

I will make earrings out of friendly plastic.
I will look at my calendar sequence to know how to make them.
My friend or I will draw a picture of how the earrings will look.
I will choose the color I want. I can choose 1, 2 or 3 colors.
My friend or I will cut out the shape I want. I can choose 1 or 2 shapes.

I will place the friendly plastic shapes(s) on foil that is placed on a cookie sheet.

I will put on the oven mitts. Then I will place the cookie sheet in the 200 degree oven. I will set the timer for 2 minutes. When the timer goes off, I will open the oven to see if the earrings are done. If they are not done, I will set the timer for 1 minute. When the timer goes off, I will put on the oven mitts, open the door and take out the cookie sheet. I will place it on a hot pad. I will ask for help if I need help.

When the friendly plastic is cool to the touch, I will take it off the foil.

I will glue one back on each earring. I can wear the earrings or give them to someone.

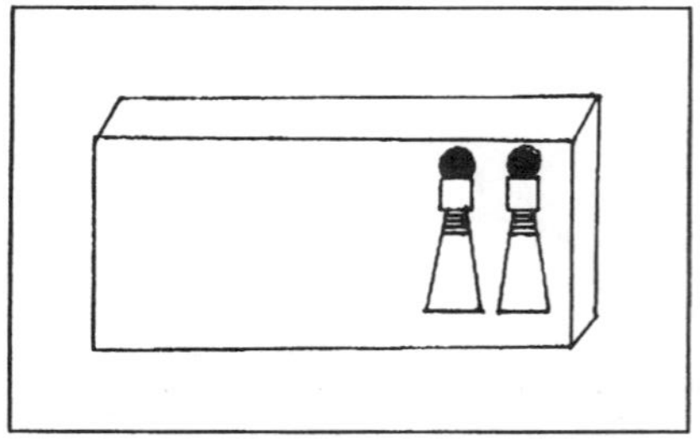

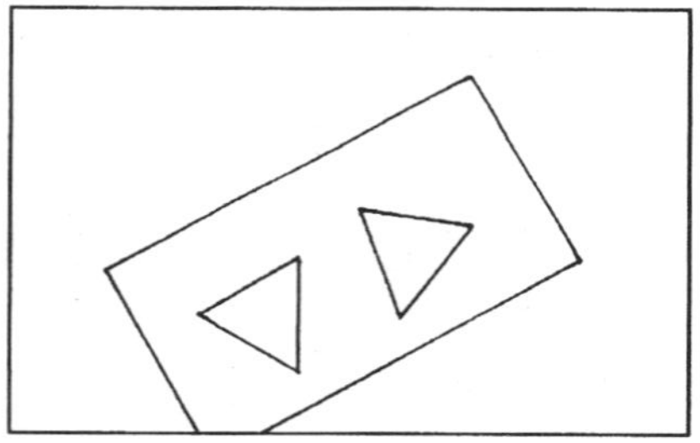

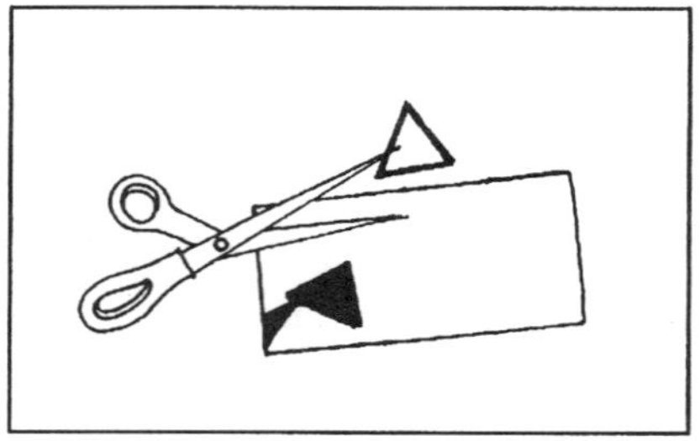

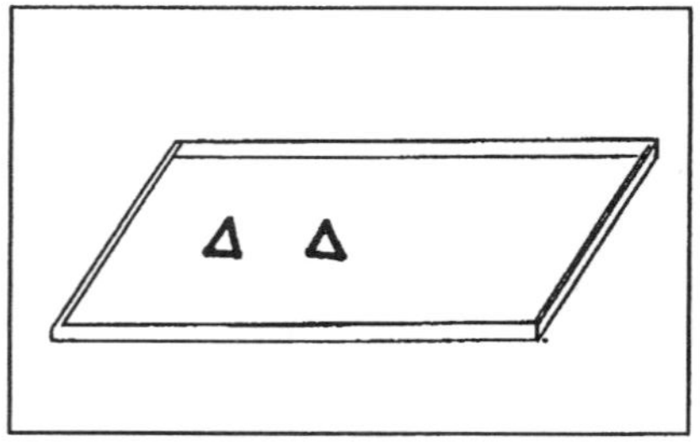

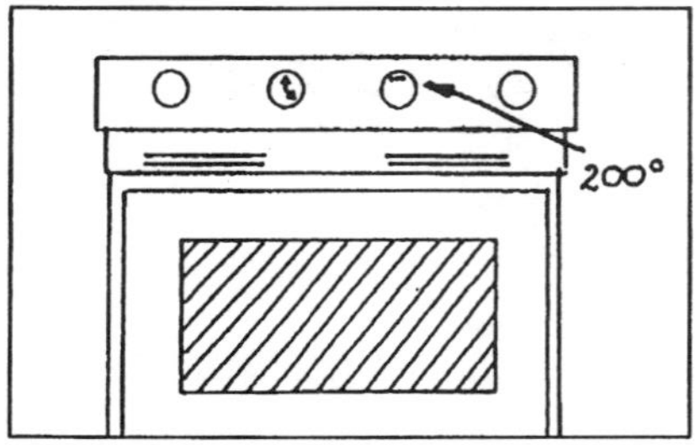

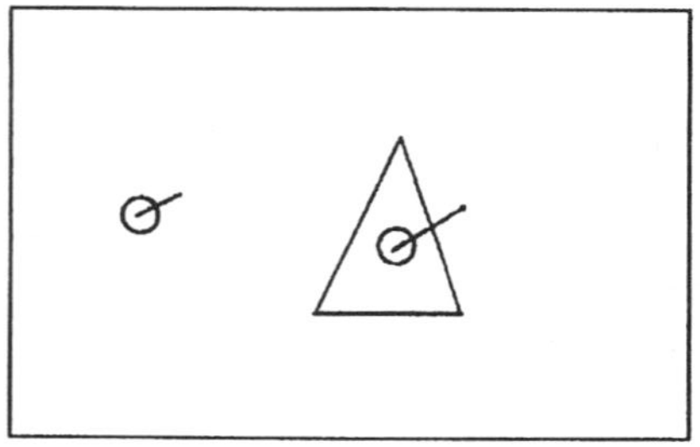

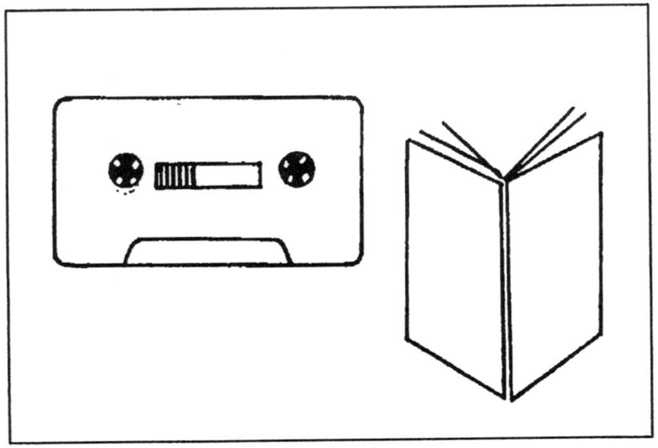

LISTENING TO BOOKS ON TAPE

Why Are We Doing This?
Individual leisure skill, encourage reading.

Materials:
Tape player
Head phones (optional)
Tapes
Books
Finished box/basket

General Rule of Thumb:
1. Have child get the tape/book and tape player (use visuals) or go to where tape player is.
2. Teach the child to:
   place tape into player
   turn player on
   place headphones on
   adjust volume
   know when tape is finished or needs to be turned over
   when to turn the page of the book.
3. Determine a way for the individual to indicate finished such as using a finished box.

Choices:
There are so many books and tapes now. Allow the individual to choose what they want to read, remembering how many items they can choose from without being overwhelmed, or they can choose from pictures.

Do It Yourself:
Allow as much independence as possible.

And Furthermore:
There are so many books and tapes available now that there is sure to be some in your individual's area of interest.

If there is not or you don't want to buy them, you can make your own. Record yourself or someone reading the book of interest. Be sure to indicate when to turn the page. Most libraries have books and tapes.

For older people, there are many books on tape. Many are abridged copies, so possible you can make your own illustrations (if not artistic use magazine pictures).

Activity Story

Its time to listen to a book being read on a tape.

I will get the tape and book and tape player.

I will go to the area where I listen to tapes.

I will put the tape in the player and push play. I will put on headphones. If it is too loud, I will turn the volume down. If I can't hear it I will turn the volume up. I can ask for help if I need it.

I will open the book. I will listen to the book being read. I will turn the page when the noise sounds.

When the tape is finished, I will push stop. I will ten push eject and take the tape out. I will put it all in the finished box.

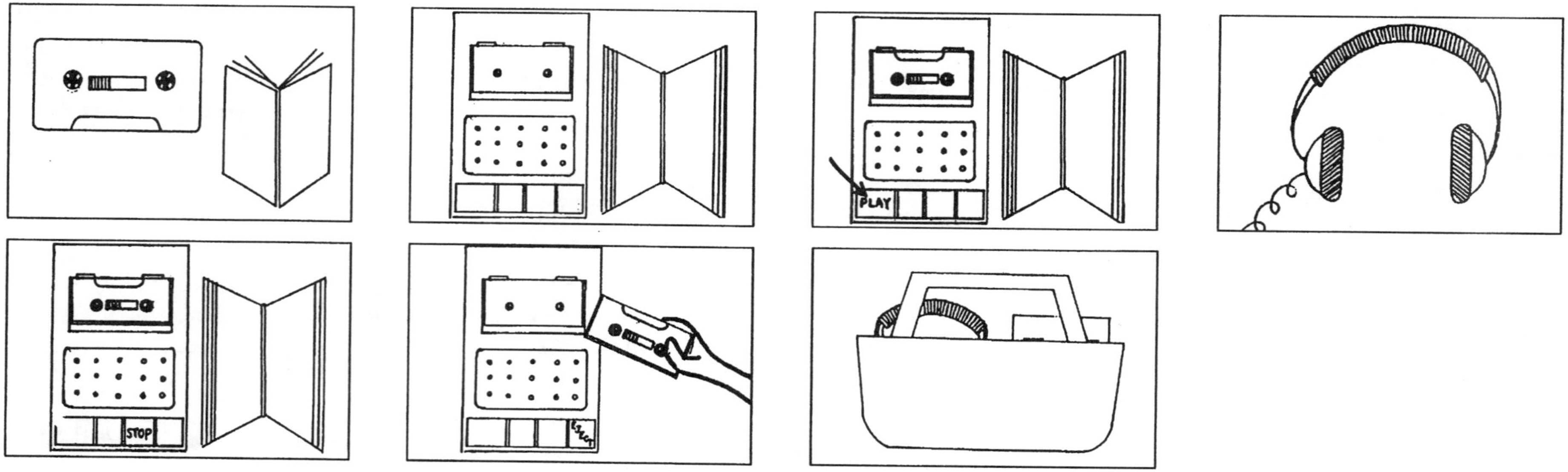

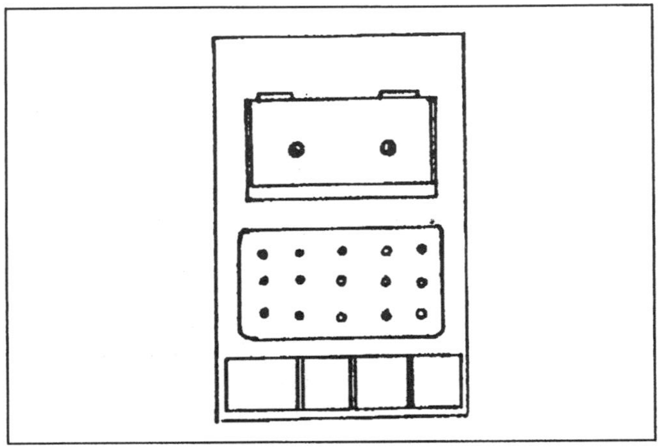

LISTENING TAPES

Why are we doing this:
To build independent leisure skills. To work on extending the ability to listen to the tape or learning how to set up, clean up, or access help.

Materials:
Cassette player
Cassette tapes
Headphones (optional)

General Rule of Thumb:
1. Prompt child to retrieve cassette player and headphones.
2. Present tapes
3. Assist as necessary:
   A. To place selected tape into player
   B. Turn the player on
   C. Place headphones on
   D. Adjust the volume
   E. Turn over tape when finished and restart
4. When finished, assist as necessary to remove tape, and put tape, player and headphones away.

Choices:
Present child with choice of tapes, making sure each one is marked with a symbol (color picture). Try different styles of music, don't assume they like yours or even kids tapes, if they are young. Try using a tape of known songs and voices. For example tape the morning circle or siblings singing at home.

Do it Yourself:
The object of this activity is independence! Rehearse problems such as when music is finished how to stop the tape, turn over or request new tape. Or how to ask for help. Also, teach how to indicate finished or more.

And Furthermore:
To accomplish independence it is necessary to teach many skills. Knowing your child is the best determining goal. Other suggested goals could be: learning to tolerate headphones, retrieving and putting away, asking for help or more, turning the player on/off.

Cautions:
Remember many children are not safe around cords, specially electrical cords. Batteries are most safe. Consider the possibility of mounting the player on a solid surface to discourage throwing or sweeping it away as some children do in frustration.

Activity Story

It's time to listen to music.

I will choose a tape. I will go to the tape player.

I will put the tape in and push play. If I need help, I will ask for help.

I can wear headphones or someone may ask me to wear headphones. When the tape is finished, I can turn it over, or I can take the tape out. What will I choose to do?

When the tape is finished, I will put the tape away.

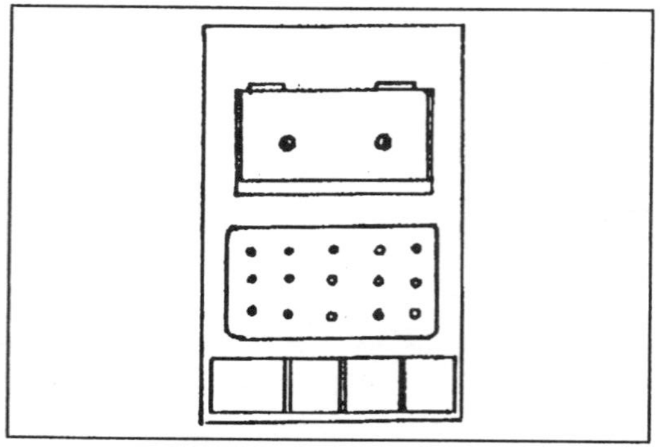

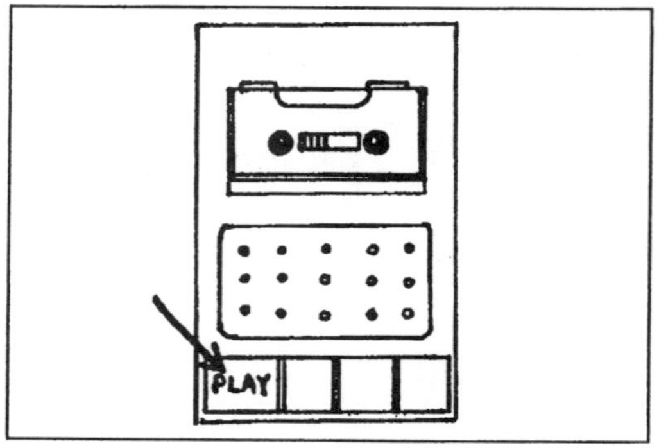

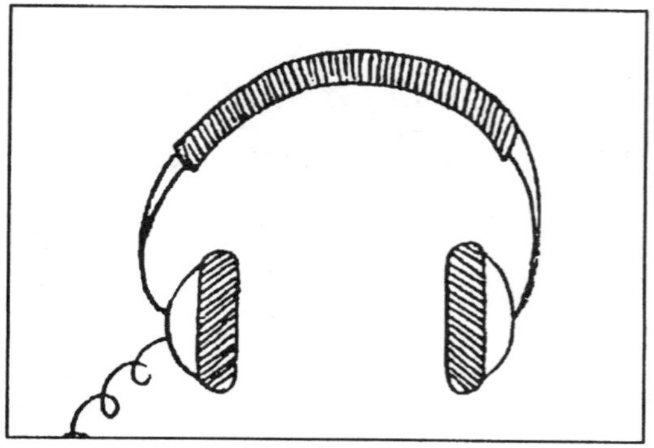

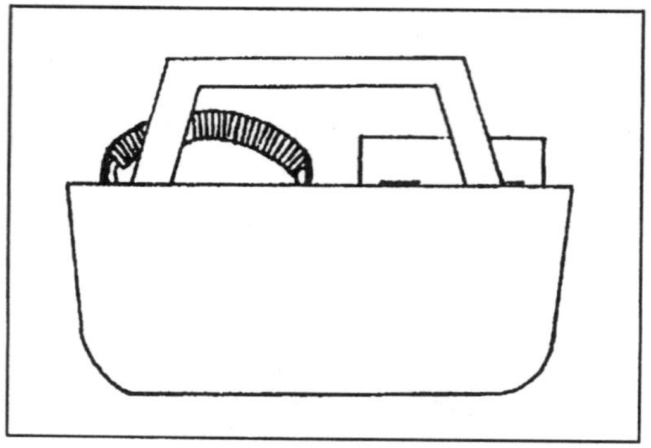

MAKING MUSIC

Why:
Noise - it's so much fun!

Materials:
Small aluminum cans such as vegetable, one end removed and edges smooth
Aluminum pie plates
Beans, rice, plastic chips, rocks and small hard objects
Tape, paper, small scooper such as a 1/4 cup

General Rule of Thumb:

1. Present the items in sequence you plan to use. For an individual working on grasping and scooping, you may want the cans as they make less mess. Those individuals who can handle distractions of beans or rice with out grabbing could use the pie plates.
2. Scoop and pour some beans, rice or rocks into the container. Place the 2nd pie plate over it or a paper cover on the can, tape in place.
3. Encourage the child to shake a variety of ways or bang on a variety of safe surfaces.

Choices:

1. If possible, present a variety of items to put in the container - be creative! Hard items work best.
2. Maybe they could choose between the can or pie plate.

And Furthermore:

Adding texture to the outside can be interesting as well. One way would be to cut a strip of clear contact that fits the pie plate or can. Tape it to the table and pull the backing off to expose the sticky side up. Encourage the child to place or spread items such as feathers, small pebbles or sand, (press firmly on) small strips of sand paper etc. Then tape the contact paper on the musical instrument. Auditory and tactile.

Activity Story

Music is so much fun. I can make my own!

First, I will choose either a can or a shiny plate. Next time I will choose again and it may be different. Then I need to choose what to pour in my container. My friend will show me what I can use.

After I choose, I pour the items in my can/plate. My friend will cover the can or plate and tape it shut. I can help if they ask.

Now I can take my shaker and make music. I may want to shake it, maybe I will shake it while listening to music. I can bang it too. I may not hurt anything when I bang it. If my friend tells me to stop, I will listen.

It is fun to make music! I can make more some other time.

Hobbies / Arts
Activity Cards

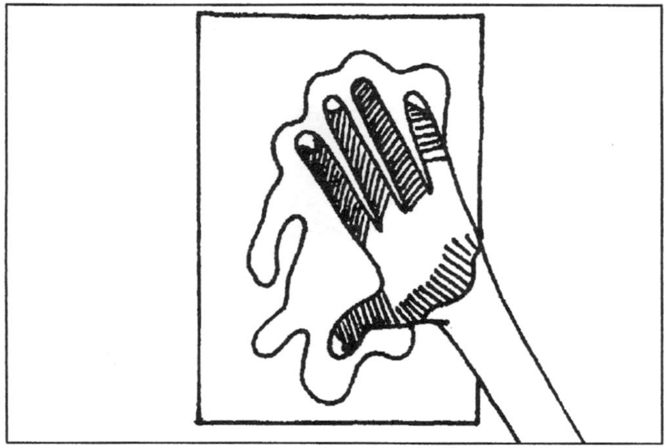

FINGER PAINTING

Why are we doing this:
To allow exploration of sensations be they soft, sticky, or hard. To work on large motor arm movements and some fine motor skills.

Materials:
Finger paints
Finger paint paper
Several of the following:
- Cornmeal
- Beans
- Rice
- Noodles
- Sand
- Cotton balls
- Sponges
- Potatoes

General Rule of Thumb:
1. Prompt the child to retrieve the necessary painting clothes. Allow time for the child to practice dressing skills.
2. Prompt the child to retrieve necessary materials such as paper and paint.
3. Present choices of paint colors, textures or paper.
4. Encourage the child to use a variety of colors, textures through gestures, verbally or modeling.
5. When finished, encourage the child to put wet artwork in a safe place to dry.
6. Assist as necessary in wash-up and removal of painting clothes.

Choices:
Allow adequate time to explore textures available, remove then present as choices. Present a variety of colors and allow the child to select from them frequently. Remember to accept appropriate opportunities to protest also.

Do it Yourself:
"Forget" an item or put some out of reach. Assist the child to ask for help. Or deliberately present the wrong item and help the child protest appropriately.

And Furthermore:
You may need to present clear "finishes" if the child has trouble indicating it. Using up an entire piece of paper has a clear visual end. Maybe using up all of the paint will be your "finish". Or set a timer.

Cautions:
Many children have difficulty determining what is okay to put into their mouths and what is not okay. Do not let the child orally explore items. Teach this is a painting time only, even if using pudding, as they will not know if it's paint or pudding the next time and may eat the paint!

Activity Story

Today I will finger paint.

Finger painting is putting paint on my hands and fingers and painting with them. I do not use a paint brush. It is OK to get paint on my fingers and hands.

I can paint a picture of something or just put paint on the paper. I can put more than one color on the paper. I only put paint on the paper.

The paint on my hands and fingers may feel funny. It may feel cold or wet or sticky. That's OK.

When I am finished painting, I will wash my hands. I will not touch my painting until it is dry.

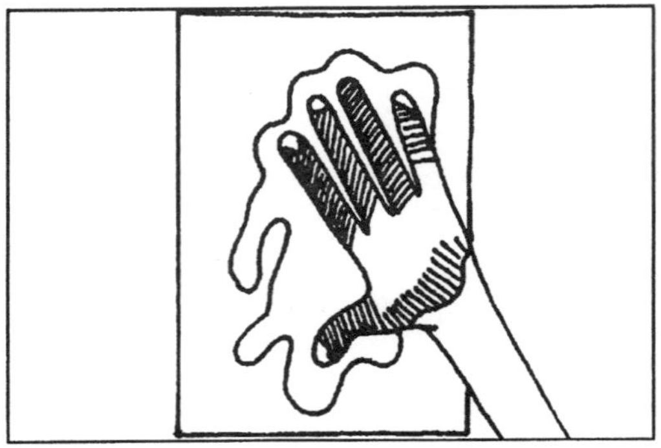

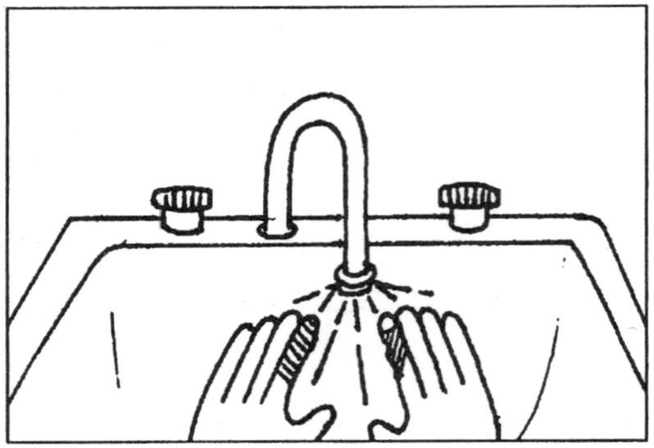

SHIRT PAINTING

Why Are We Doing This?
Creativity; Sense of accomplishment

Materials:
T-shirt or sweatshirt
Fabric Paint brush
Stencils or shapes (optional)

General Rule of Thumb:
1. Pick a shirt to paint. It could be an old one if you want to experiment. Put wax paper or cardboard in the shirt so the paint does not go through to the back side.
2. Either use paint tubes or brush and paint if too difficult to squeeze tube and paint.
3. Use stencils, draw design on, or free paint.
4. Allow paint to dry.

Choices:
Lots of choices here. What colors? What picture, shapes or stencil?

Do It Yourself:
Refrain yourself from wanting a perfect picture. This is the individual's creativity and picture.

Cautions:
Watch if you have an "eater" or tactile defensive individual.

Activity Story

Today we are painting a shirt.

There will be wax paper or cardboard inside the shirt and the shirt will be on the table.

I can paint any picture and use any colors I want.

I will not touch the paint on the shirt until it is dry.

The paint will be dry when I can wear the shirt.

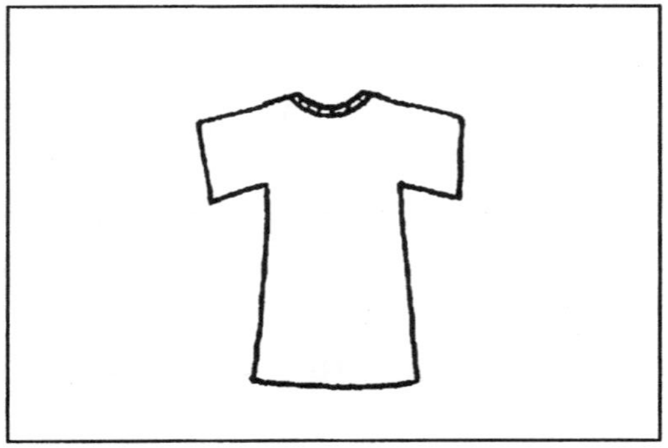

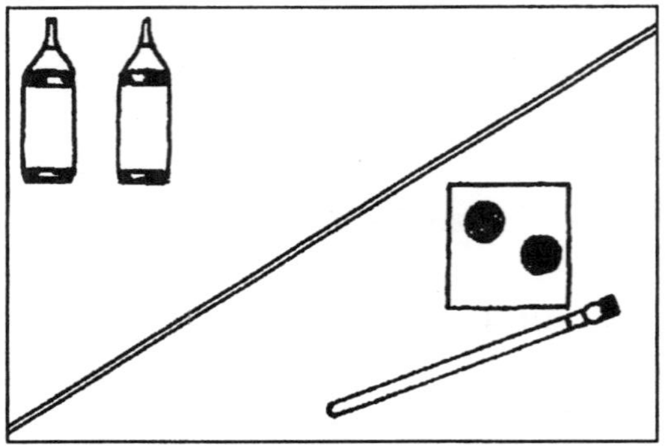

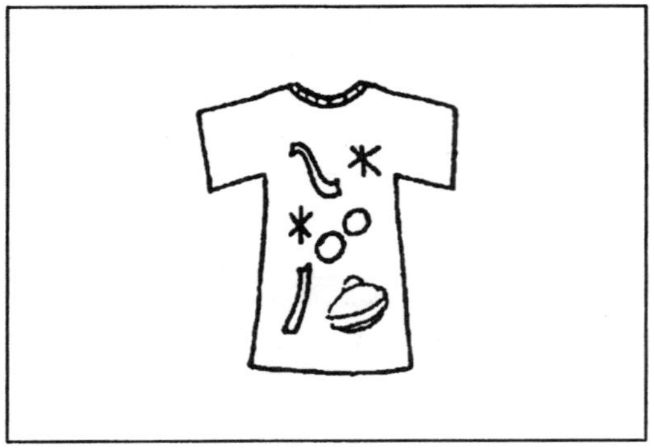

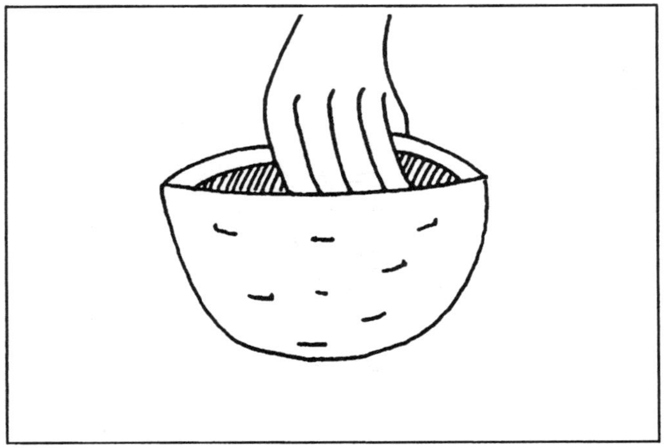

POTTERY - PINCH POT

Why Are We Doing This?
Creativity; sense of accomplishment (finished product), fine motor skills.

Materials:
1 pound clay

General Rule of Thumb:
1. Give your child clay and have them roll it into a ball.
2. Have child start making a hole in the middle of the clay by using his/her thumb.
3. Decide how the child will know when he is done with the pinch pot.
4. Place the pinch pot on a cookie sheet either to dry or to put in oven. Set oven to 350 degrees - Can your child do that?
5. Bake for 1 hour. Set timer so child will know passing of time.
6. Take out and let it cool. Again set the timer so the child knows when they can touch it.

Choices:
Let child decide what they want to do with the pinch pot (present? something to hold keepsakes?)

Do It Yourself:
Independence is important. Show a picture. Sequence to show steps. Or have a peer or yourself do one at the same time.

Can he/she use the oven and be safe? Can he/she set the oven?

And Furthermore:
Always use oven mitts when putting in and taking out of oven.

Cautions:
Watch carefully if your child/student puts things in his/her mouth or is tactually defensive. Also caution with the oven if using baker's clay.

Activity Story:

Today we will make a pinch pot out of clay. A pinch pot is a bowl you make out of clay by pinching the clay and shaping it into a bowl.

First, I will roll the clay into a ball. I can do this by squeezing it and rolling it on the table.

I will press my thumb into the center of the clay ball to make a hole. At the same time I will squeeze the clay with my fingers. I will keep doing this all the way around the clay. This way the hole gets bigger and starts to look like a pot or bowl. I will squeeze the sides until they are 1/4 inch thick. Someone will tell me when it is the right size.

I will continue to shape the bowl by using my fingers or whole fist.

I will put my bowl on a cookie sheet. I will set the oven to bake at 350 degrees. I will put the cookie sheet in the oven. It will bake for one hour (see recipe in Appendix). When it is done I can give my bowl to someone, keep it, put things in it.

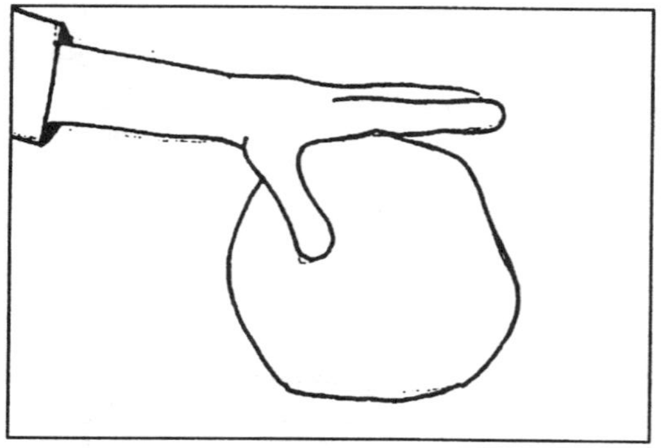

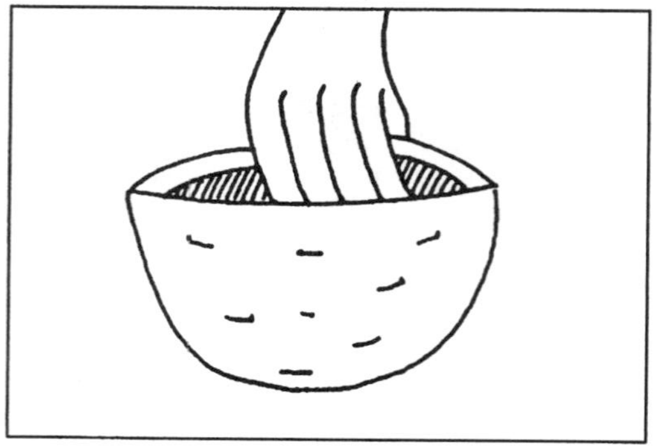

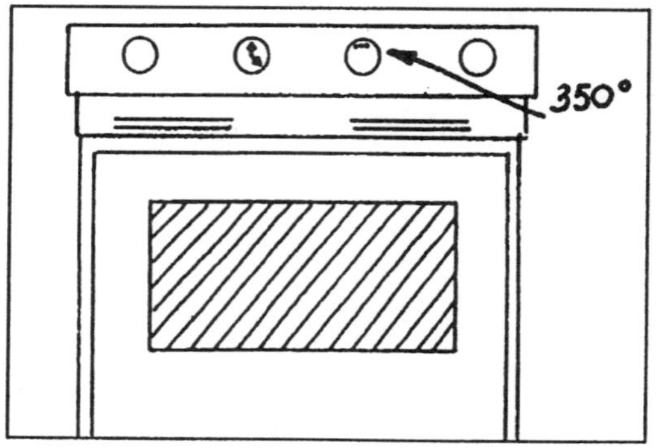

POTTERY - CANDLE HOLDER

Why Are We Doing This?
Creativity; finished project; following a sequence to complete a project. Fun! Some measuring skills.

Materials:
Clay - 1 lb. + 1/4 lb.
Wire (to cut the clay)

General Rule of Thumb:

1. Cut one pound of clay in half with a wire.
2. Give your child one half of the clay and have him/her form the cup part of the candle holder. He/she can use his/her thumb.
3. Once the cup part is done, give the other half of the clay and have him/her flatten it with the heel of his/her hand to make the base.
4. The cup part goes on the base. The two pieces need to be pinched together. If your child does not understand how to do this, show him/her how or do it for them. Smooth out the base.
5. Take more clay to make the handle. Have child roll into a 6" by 3/4" strip. (See Furthermore for measurement ideas).
6. Attach one end of the strip to the holder and one end to the base. Pinch together.
7. Check the size of the holder by putting a candle in it. You wouldn't want the finished product to not fit!
8. Place on a cookie sheet and put it into a 350 degree oven for an hour. Set a timer or show on the clock when the holder will be done.
9. Cool completely - again set a timer or clock.

Choices:

Do It Yourself:
Give your child the picture sequence to follow. Also, do one yourself or a peer do one with your child.

A finished product might help your child see the purpose in doing this product.

And Furthermore:
For measuring, use a ruler or if your child/student does not understand a rule cut a string to measure by.

Activity Story:

Today we will make a candle holder. A candle holder holds a candle up so it won't fall over.

I will roll the clay into a ball. I will ask someone to cut the ball in half so there are two pieces.

I will pick up one piece and put in my thumb in the middle to make a hole to put the candle in.

Once the one piece has a hole I will put that piece down. I will then pound the other piece so that it is flat. I can do this with my hand.

I will then place the piece with the hole in it on top of the flat piece. To keep the pieces together I will pinch the clay together. I will make sure it is smooth or straight by touching it with my finger. Are there any bumps? If there are bumps, press them down with my finger.

I will take another piece of clay and roll it into a 6" long piece. I will place one end on the flat piece and pinch it into place. I will place the other end to the holder piece. I will make a loop.

I will let it dry for _____ or bake it. I can ask someone when it is dry or look at my calendar. When it is dry, I can put a candle in it.

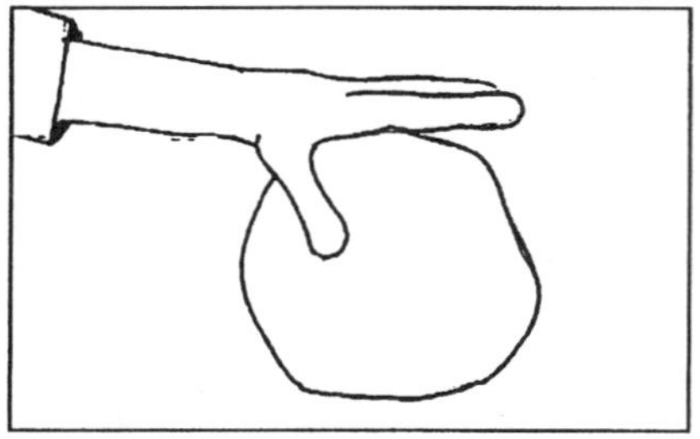

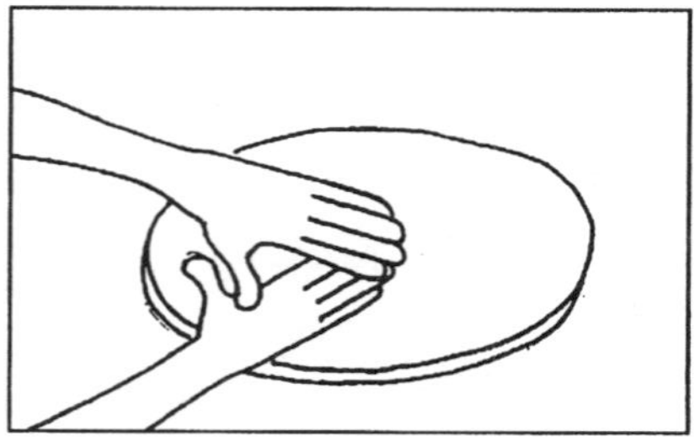

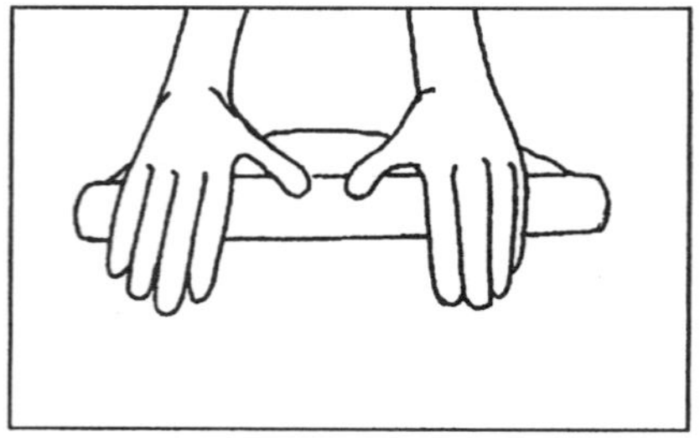

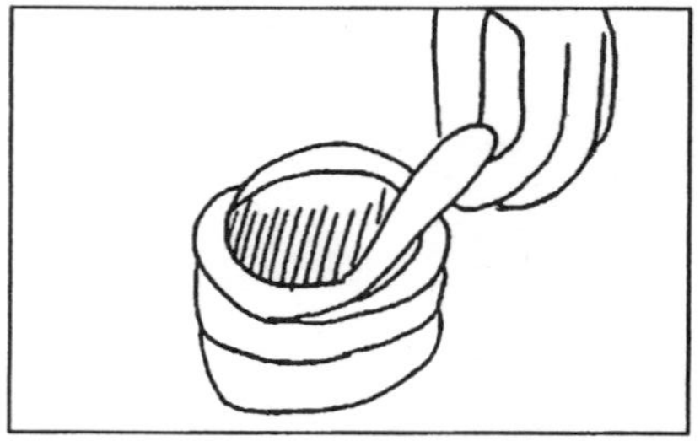

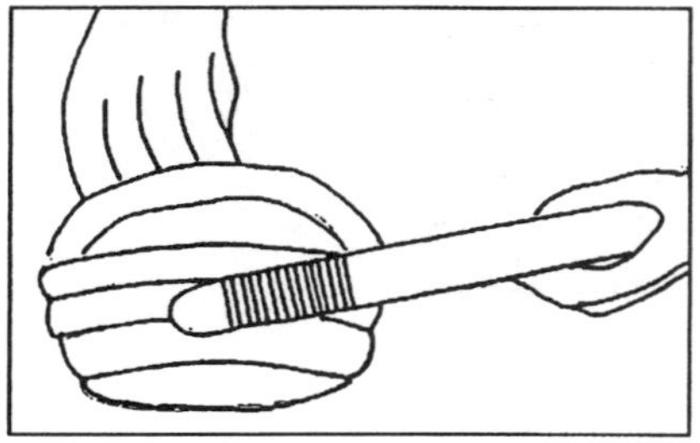

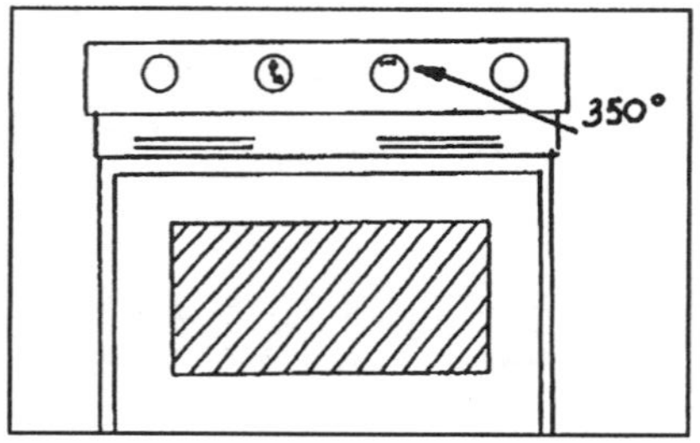

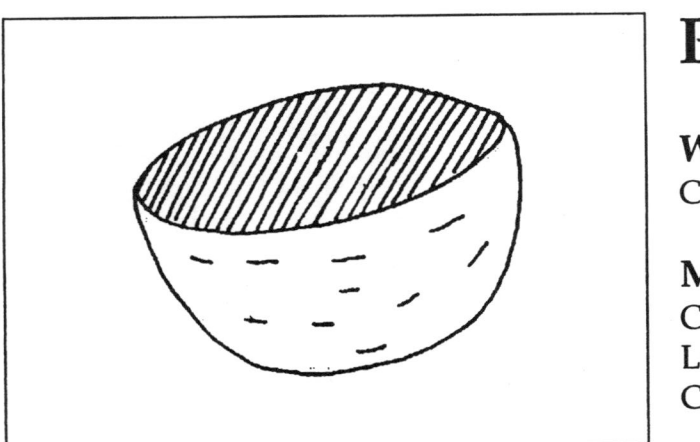

POTTERY: COIL POT

Why Are We Doing This?
Creativity; sense of completion.

Materials:
Clay: 1/2 lb. piece, additional piece
Lazy Susan with paper towel on it
Craft stick with string wrapped around it.

General Rule of Thumb:
1. Give child 1 piece of clay. Have him/her flatten that piece into a circle. Give a visual circle of how to make it.
2. Give him/her another piece of clay. Give him/her pieces of clay to roll into "snakes." Again, give a visual of how long to make the snakes.
3. After the child has made enough snakes, have him/her start coiling the snakes on the base to make the pot. Pinch each coil to the one below to form a seam.
4. Wrap a string around a craft stick and have the child pat the outside of the pot to give it a textured look.
5. Have child smooth the inside of the pot with his/her fingers.
6. Place pot on cookie sheet. Set oven to bake at 350 degrees. Allow child to do this if possible. Place cookie sheet in the oven and bake for 1 hour. Set a timer to show passing of time, or show on clock when done.
7. Take pot out of oven and let cool. Again, set a timer or show on clock when cool.

Choices:
Let child choose how big, within reason to make his/her pot.

Do It Yourself:
Let the child complete as much as possible.

Activity Story

Today we will make a coil pot out of clay. A coil pot is made out of several pieces of clay.

First, I will take one piece of clay and make it flat by pushing on it. I will place it on the paper towel that is on the lazy Susan. This is called the base.

I will then shape more clay into a snakelike strip by rolling it on the table with the palms of my hands. They will be 7" to 10" long.

Coil or wrap the strip around the edge of the flat piece or base. I will pinch the edges around so there are no holes. I will continue to make strips and place them on top of the others.

I will make it as high as I want.

When I have made the pot as high as I want I will take the stick with the string wrapped around it and pat the outside of the pot.

I will make sure the inside of the pot is smooth by rubbing it with my fingers

[*where: I will put it in the oven or ask for help.]

I will cook it for _____ . I can ask someone when it is dry or look at my calendar.

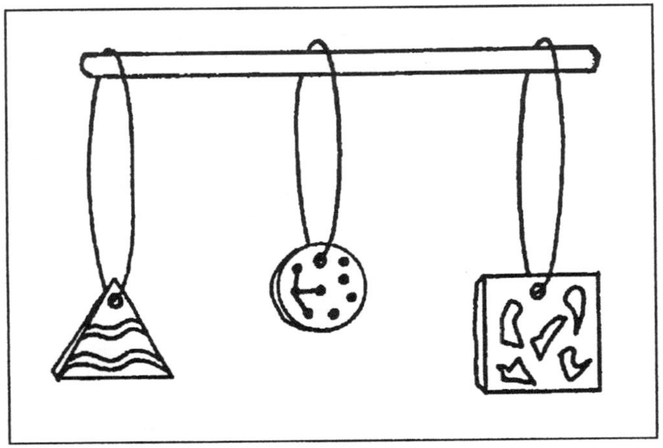

POTTERY - WIND CHIME

Why Are We Doing This?
Create something that gives auditory and visual feedback; lots of choice making.

Materials:
Clay
Chimes
Shapes or cookie cutters
Rolling pin
Knife (dull)
2 feet 1/4" doweling
Decorations (such as beads, shells, feathers, etc.)
String

General Rule of Thumb:
1. Have child draw and cut out shapes or choose cookie cutters to make the shapes (see choices).
2. Have child cut out the shapes out of the clay.
3. In each shape make a small hole at the top for the string.
4. Place on a cookie sheet and place it in the 350 degree oven. Bake for 1 hour (see recipe in Appendix). Remove and let cool. Set timer or show on clock the passing of time.
5. After cooling, allow child to decorate the shapes.
6. Tie a chime to each string. Place string through the holes and tie to a dowel.
7. Where will the child hang it?

Choices:
So many choices! Make own shapes or use cookie cutters? What shapes? What decorations to use, if any? How many shapes to make? If your child/student cannot make this many choices, cut down on the choices.

Do It Yourself:
Allow as much independence as possible or do partial and allow child/student to finish.

And Furthermore:

Cautions:
Watch the knife and scissors. Even the doweling can be dangerous.

Activity Story

Today we will make a wind chime. A wind chime is shapes hanging by string that if placed in the wind will make a nice noise.

I will roll out my clay with a rolling pin to make it flat.

I will make shapes out of paper. I can make circles or animals or anything I want. I will cut the shapes out and place them on the clay. I will use the knife to cut around the shape. I will be careful with the knife. Or, I will ask an adult to cut out the shapes with the knife. Or, I will use cookie cutters to cut out shapes.

I put a hole in the top of the shape so when the clay is dry/baked I can put string in the hole to hang the shape.

After the shapes are dry/baked, I will decorate them by gluing (sequins, feathers, beads) on the shapes.

I will cut string.

I will put the string through the holes in the shapes and tie the string to the stick. I will do this with all the shapes. I will put a chime on each shape.

I can hold or hang the wind chime up. When the wind blows on it, it will make a nice noise. If there is no wind, I can blow on it to make the noise.

Get clay
Roll clay flat

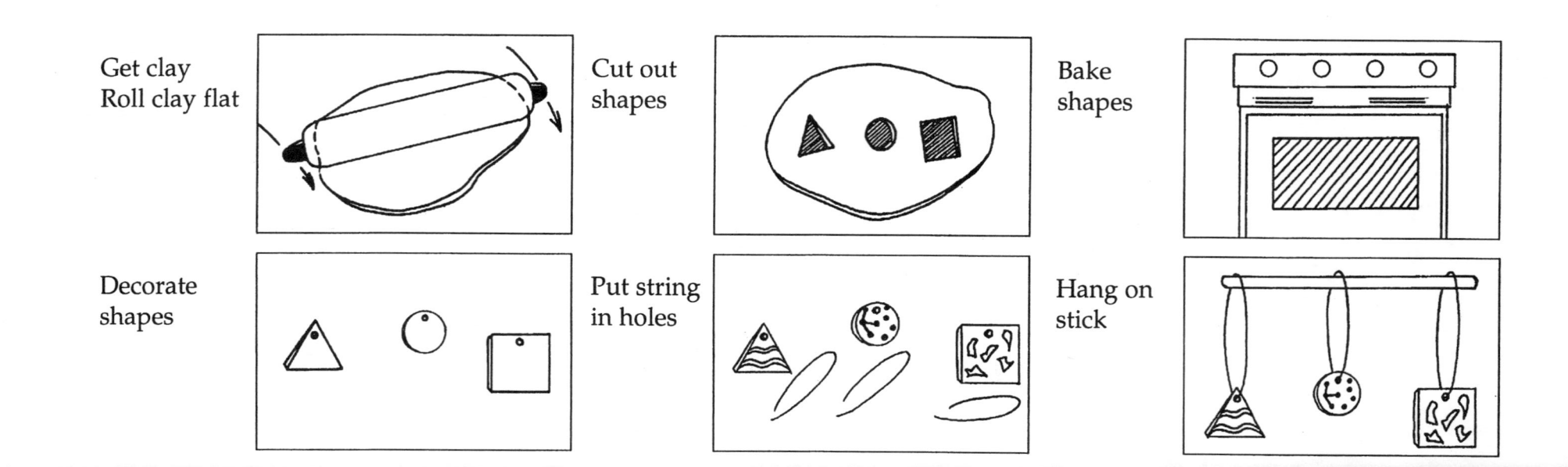

Cut out shapes

Bake shapes

Decorate shapes

Put string in holes

Hang on stick

STUFF IT IN

Why:
Good finger exercises and pretty things to see!

Materials:
Clear acetate paper (found at craft stores)
Stapler
Fillers: colored tissue, feathers, beans, cotton balls etc.
Hole punch and yarn

General Rule of Thumb:
1. Cut out desired shapes of acetate such as animals - a chick or fish, or a snowman. Staple around the edges close enough to keep things from falling through. Be sure to leave an opening.
2. Assist as necessary to hold the shape and have the individual grab items and stuff in. Cotton balls in a snowman shape, feathers in a chick or duck, or tissue in a fish. Staple shut when done.
3. Using a hole punch, make a hole to hang it by. String the yarn through and hang from a high place!

Choices:
What shape to use, what to fill the shape with and where to hang it!

Do it Yourself:
Encourage independence in stuffing. Reach, grasp, release in are good skills to practice. Be careful not to help too much. Give the individual time to think about it and mix your help with points, taps, physical assist, verbal or combinations of these. Otherwise, the individual may think part of the task is you taking their hand to pick up and stuff.

And Furthermore:
So you have lot's of hanging shapes? Grab some paper towel rolls and start swinging! Who can hit the snowman? Two points for the bunny!!

Activity Story

Today I will make pretty shapes. First, I will decide what shape to make. I may make an animal, a snowman, a bus or anything I want. I will tell my friend what shape I want and they will help me cut it out.

After I cut out my shape two times I will use a stapler to staple around the edges. My friend will help me when I need it.

Next, I will choose what to put in the shape. It could be feathers, cotton, beans, tissue paper. My friend will help me with my choices.

I will fill my shape with my choices. Then, I will staple it shut.

I can give my shape as a gift or keep it. I can hang my shape up or keep it on a table.

I like making pretty shapes. It's fun to work hard and see a pretty shape!

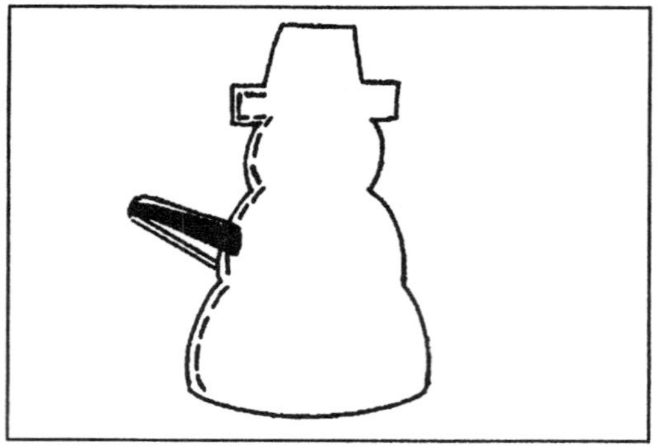

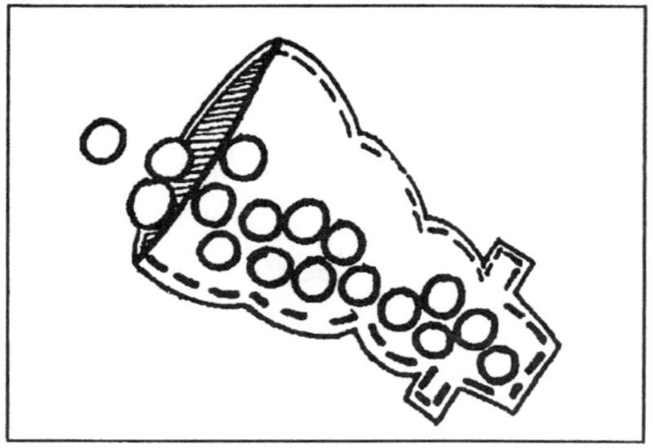

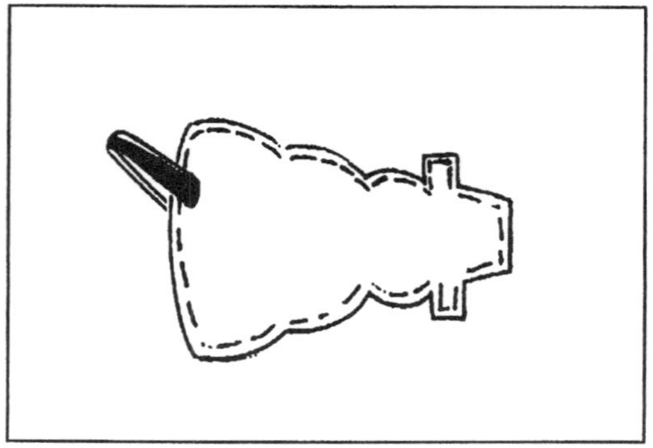

Other Activity Cards

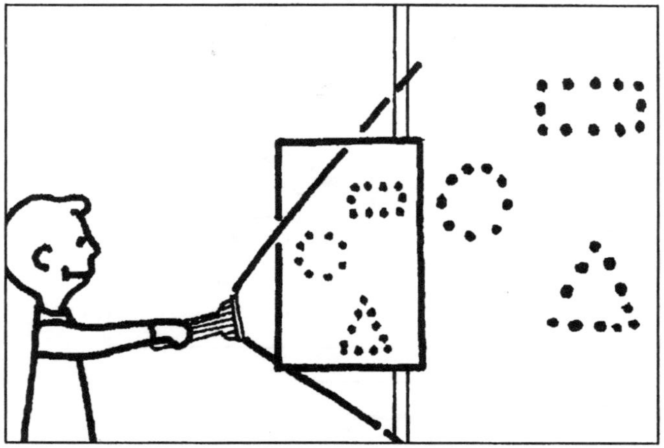

WHAT GOES THERE:

Why are we doing this?
To explore visual attending and to practice cause and effect.

Materials:
Heavy paper
Sharp pointed utensil or scissors
Flashlight or stationary light
Optional box and tissue paper

General Rule of Thumb:
1. Assist child to draw simple shape on paper.
2. Adult needs to poke uniform holes around the shape.
3. Assist child in holding paper in front of flashlight or stationary light.
4. Direct the stencil against a wall, a box, or different textured surfaces. Move the paper and the flashlight. Watch what happens.
5. Try cutting the whole shape out and covering the opening with tissue paper. What happens?
6. When finished, take the stencil to art. How about coloring it?

Choices:
Allow choice of shapes as much as possible and choice of lights.

Do it Yourself:
Encourage the child to ask for help with the light or paper to keep frustration down.

And Furthermore:
Play with the light. Of it's not dark where does the shape go? If the shape is cut out what happens? What about if it's covered with tissue? Remember to encourage language through experiences!

Cautions:
Flashing the light will entrance some children. Be careful it doesn't become the focus and possibly set off a seizure.

Activity Story

I am going to make a pattern in paper that will be fun to shine light through.

First I will take paper and draw shapes on it. I can choose any shape I want.

Next, I will poke holes around the shapes on the paper. If I need help to do this, I will ask my friend.

I will shine the flashlight behind the paper. I will want to point the light and paper at a wall so I can see the light shine through the paper.

I can make the shapes move on the wall. I can make the light move by turning it off and on.

When play is finished, I will put the paper away. I will be sure to turn off the flashlight.

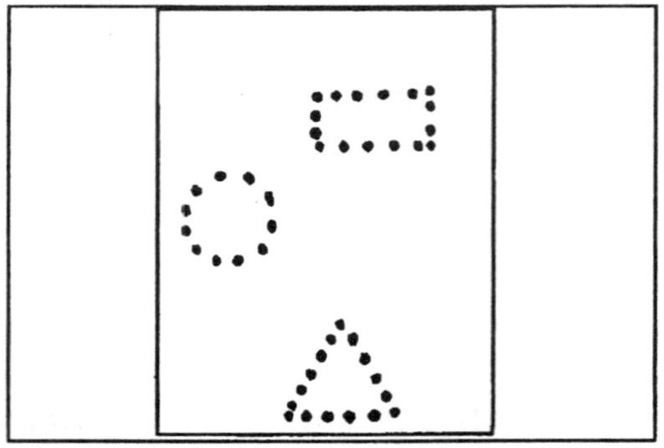

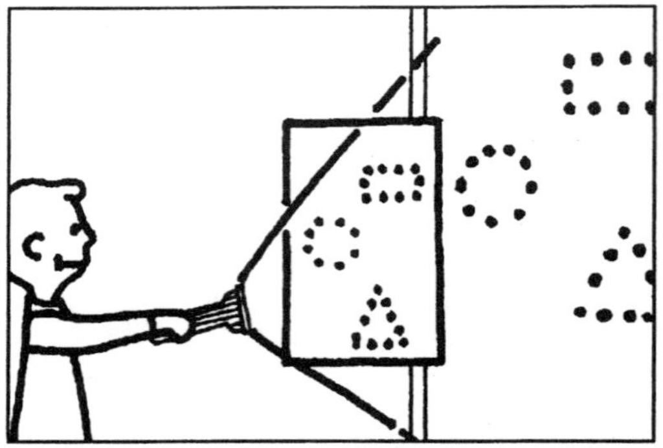

FLAPPING IN THE WIND

Why are we doing this?
Using a process which involves fine motor tasks to create a pleasurable sensory experience.

Materials:
Paint sticks
Shiny paper such as mylar or foil cut 1/2 the length of the sticks and 6" wide
Glue
Scissors
Fan or hair dryer

General Rule of Thumb:
1. Assist as necessary for the child to create fringe on one long side of the paper by either cutting or ripping. Ripping might be best accomplished after step 2, however.
2. Apply glue to un-torn edge and place on edge of paint stick.
3. Allow to dry for a few minutes.
4. If possible, use the fan/hair dryer to blow on the flapper and/or child.
5. Encourage the child to blow and explore what the wind does.

Choices:
Allow choice of paper or color from the child. If possible provide choice of fan or hair dryer. If only one is used, stop and start it periodically so child practices indicating "more" or "on".

Do it Yourself:
This task is not meant to be independent as it uses scissors and the fan/hair dryer. But once made, it could be an independent leisure choice without the fan/hair dryer. Explore to see if it would be a choice for a child and would occupy them for a period of time.

And Furthermore:
Don't forget that the soft flutter of the flapper is fun to feel on the body; maybe the face, arms, legs, etc. Be creative in the sensory options!!

Cautions:
Provide close adult supervision with the fan or hair dryer and the scissors if they are used. Remember many students with autism have little or no sense of danger so it is the caregiver's responsibility!!

Activity Story

Today I will make a pom pom that I can shake and flap. I can make it out of paper that is shiny or any color I want.

First, I pick the sheet of paper I want.

I will put glue on the stick. The glue only goes on one side from the top to the handle.

I lay the paper on the glue. If I lay one end of the paper on the glue, the pom pom will have long pieces. If I lay the paper on the middle, the pom pom will have short pieces.

When the glue is dry, I will cut or tear the ends of the paper. I will have to be careful not to tear the paper off.

If I tear the paper off, it's okay. I can get help to tape it back on.

After I tear/cut the paper, I can shake the pom pom. I can shake it on my face, my arm or leg. I may not put it in my mouth.

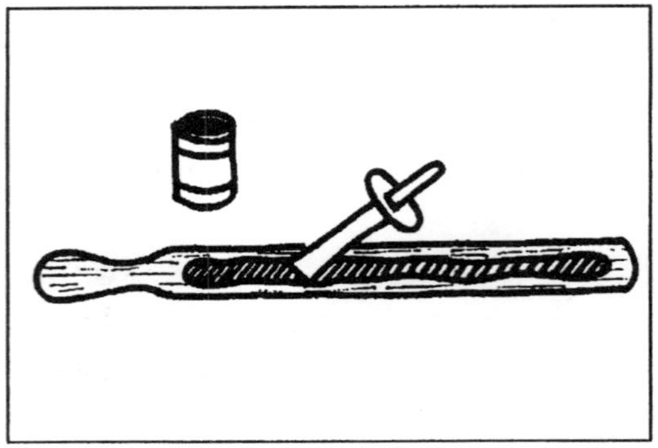

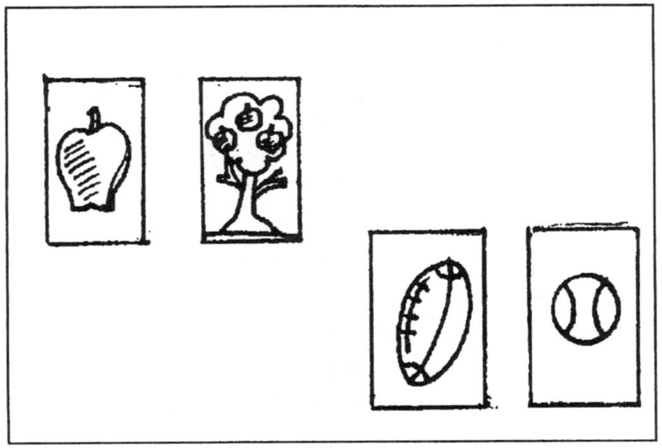

WHAT DOES IT FEEL LIKE?

Why are we doing this:
To explore a variety of textures and how it feels to pour, dump and squeeze. Movement is the opportunity to learn and build on language through experiences.

Materials:
Plastic bins with lids
Variety of:
Beans
Rice
Cornmeal
Sand
Macaroni
Oobla or sticky balls

Variety of utensils to pour and fill:
Spoons
Cups, buckets
Sifter, funnel

General Rule of Thumb:
1. Present bins with one texture per bin. (The lids can be useful for storage or use 2 or 3 bins and store the textures in bags.)
2. Present toys such as cups and spoons.
3. Assist as necessary for child to feel and discover the textures. Pour and fill, do they make noise?
4. Be sure to talk about what they are doing. Let them hear words as they feel the action.
5. Assist as necessary to indicate you are finished and put away the bins.

Choices:
Present the bins two or three at a time to encourage choice making but encourage variety and don't let them get stuck on one. Encourage them to become open to all the textures for exploration. Allow choice in the utensils used also!

Do it Yourself:
Encourage the child to feel the textures as much as possible, even try sticking your feet in the bin of beans. Encourage play between students or between yourself and the child. You pour on his arm, he pours on yours - make up games!

And Furthermore:
Textures are fun to explore. It can be helpful to put a big sheet on the floor and put the bins in the middle. Then when you're done, shake the sheet off and you're ready for the next time.

Cautions:
Be careful the textures are explored but NOT eaten or put into the mouth where they can be choked on.

Activity Story

It is fun to put your hands into things that feel different.

I will put my hands into buckets. Some buckets hold hard things, soft things even squishy things.

If I don't like my hands in a bucket, I can tell my friend. We will put the bucket away.

When I play in the buckets, I may scoop, pour, squeeze or even rub between my hands. I may not put anything in my mouth or throw.

When I am finished playing in the buckets, I will put the topes on, put them on the shelf. I will then wash my hands.

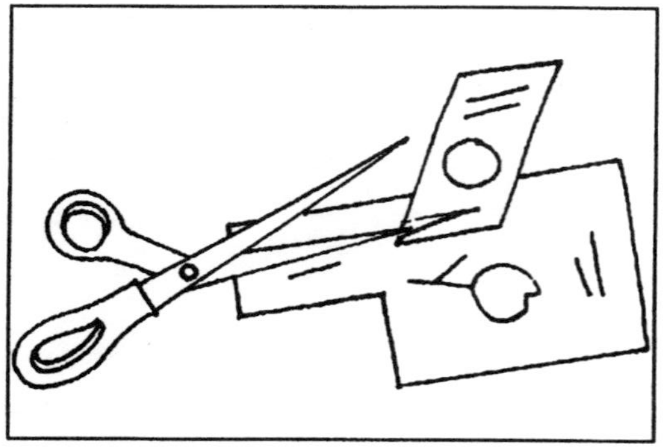

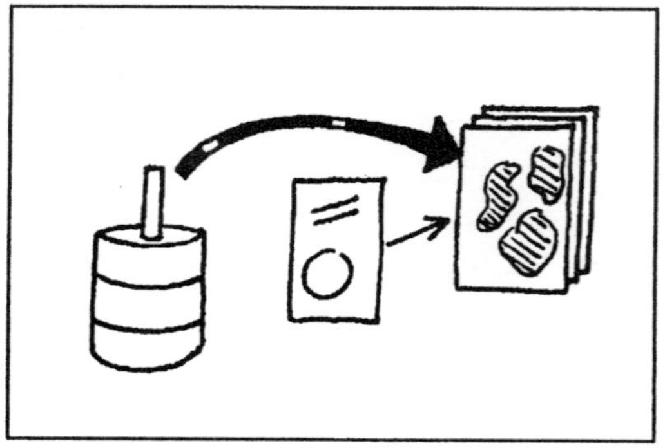

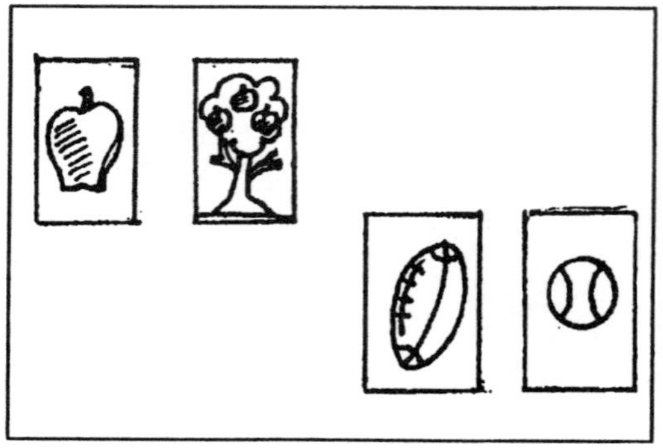

SQUISHY SQUASHY FUN

Why are we doing this:
To explore different squishy feelings as well as warm and cold feelings. It provides an end product that can be reused.

Materials:
Plastic baggies; heavy duty, resealable type
Duct tape if regular baggies are used
Corn syrup; 1 cup per bag
Any soft colored items:
    Glitter
    Cotton Balls
    Sequins

Measuring cup
Containers for hot and cold water

General Rule of Thumb:
1. Retrieve necessary materials.
2. Assist as necessary to measure 1 cup of corn syrup into a baggie.
3. Present choices of objects and assist as necessary to place in baggie
4. Allow exploration time for the child to squish the items found.
5. Present the two containers of hot and cold water. Assist the child in experiencing warm and cold, by placing the baggies in each for a minute or so and then feeling the baggies.
6. Cooking oil and paint can also be placed in a baggie to make unusual patters.

Choices:
After exploration present containers of water for repeated choices, remember to offer choices of what they want in their bags. If this is a repeat activity, the choices should increase. Also encourage some different items in the bag or use paint and oil this time. Encourage variety!

Do it Yourself:
Allow adequate exploration as there are many experiences in the squishy textures of syrup/oil and sparkly things or oil/paint designs. The warmth and coolness can be felt with more than just fingers, however see caution note.

And Furthermore:
Remember the "wholistic" learning style of the children. You can work on measuring, pouring, scooping or fine motor manipulation of picking items to put in the bag. But show them all these parts create the end goal.

Cautions:
Be careful the child does not bit the bag as many kids explore with their mouths first!

Activity Story

Today I will be filling a bag with syrup to make a squishy bag. A squishy bag feels soft and I can push on it with my hands.

First I will pour from a cup into the bag.

I can choose to put pieces of soft yarn in my bag. Some of the pieces maybe shiny. I will choose five pieces to put in.

My friend will put tape on my bag so the syrup does not come back out.

I can squish my bag with my hands. I can put by bag in hot or cold water to make it feel different.

I cannot break my bag open. I must leave it closed.

When play is finished, I will put my bag away. I will wash my hands.

STICK IT ON!

Why are we doing this?
To explore textures and practice finger exercises.

Materials:
Small crumpled pieces of tissue
Large animal shapes cut out of poster board
Glue poured into a small container such as a aluminum art or pie pan

General Rule of Thumb:
1. Place the items in a sequence - tissue, glue, cut out
2. Assist as necessary to grasp one piece of tissue, dip in glue and place on cut out. If you place the cut out on wax paper, accuracy won't matter as when you lift the cut out up it will still look like the animal.

Choices:
Choices could be the animal shape, color of cut out or color of tissue paper.

Do it Yourself:
Be careful, the individual doesn't expect you to guide them through the sequence. Encourage independence by varying prompts with points, taps, verbal or a combination. And hardest yet - WAIT for them to think about it. There is no speed required.

You may want to make tearing and crumpling the tissue paper a separate activity. It's good finger exercise too.

And Furthermore:
You can vary the activity by glueing feathers or other items. Maybe use clear contact cut in shapes if glue is too hard. Tape the contact paper on the table and peel back to expose the sticky side. Stick away!

Activity Story

Today I will make pretty animal shapes. It is fun to work with paper and glue.

My friend will give me paper that is in shape of animals! I will choose which animal I want to make pretty. I will choose which color of little paper I will use.

I take a piece of little colored paper and dip it in the glue. I put the paper on my animal. I can put many pieces or not many. I can put them anywhere I choose on my animal.

When I have put as many little pieces as I want, I will leave the picture for the glue to dry. When the glue is dry, I can hang my animal up, give it to Mom or Dad.

It's fun to make animal shapes!

PICK A FEEL

Why are we doing this:

Materials:
Fabric scraps
Cardboard cut 8 1/2 x 11 with a hole punched in upper left corner
Visqueen of clear plastic cut as described in step 2
Glue
Metal ring

General Rule of Thumb:

1. Present an assortment of fabrics cut into different shapes. (If the child is good with and safe with scissors, he/she may want to cut the fabric themselves)
2. Present the child with precut pieces of cardboard and Visqueen (clear plastic).
3. Assist as necessary to glue the Visqueen to the cardboard. The Visqueen should be cut 1/2 the length of the cardboard and 1 1/2 inches wider than the fabric piece so when the Visqueen is glued on three sides, there is room to allow the fabric to slide into the pocket.
4. Allow time for the child to explore favorite textures. Select fabric to put in pockets.

Do it Yourself:
There are many fine motor skills to work on in this task, but remember being able to ask for help and knowing when to ask is important too! If a texture is not preferred work on how to protest appropriately.

And Furthermore:
Tactile exploration is very important for children with sensory processing scrambles. Encourage the exploration of as many different textures as possible. Increase the tolerance of the less preferred textures. Remember to explore the feel of the textures on the arms, legs, face, etc.

Cautions:
Do not use scissors with all kids and watch the glue. It's fun to feel it's texture but remember the goal is to glue the Visqueen, not the mouth!

Choices:
Choices are built into this activity but it's a good time to practice the ability to indicate clearly. Don't forget to represent the choices and remind them of all the choices in their book, not the same one over and over.

Activity Story

Today I will make a book and put different fabrics or material in it. This kind of book is called a scrap book. Fabric or material is cloth like your clothes or blankets. Some fabric or material feels soft, some feel rough.

At first, the book will be empty with only pockets on each page.

I will choose what material I want to put in the book. I will try to put different feel material in it. I will put one piece of material in each pocket.

I can ask for help if I need it.

This scrap book is for me to look at and touch the different feels of the material or fabric. When I want to touch the material, I will take the material out of the pocket, touch it and then put it back in the pocket. Then I can choose another material.

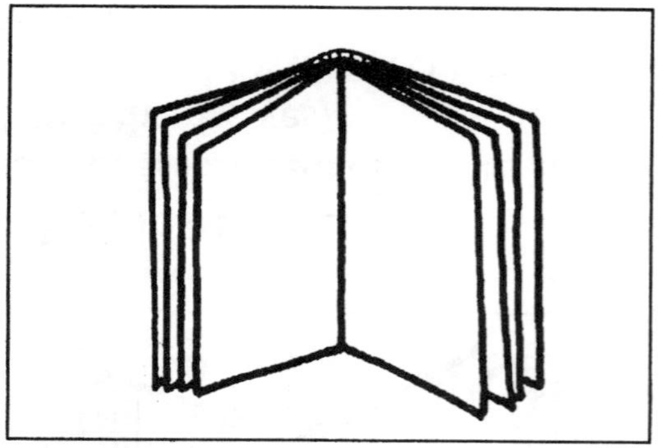

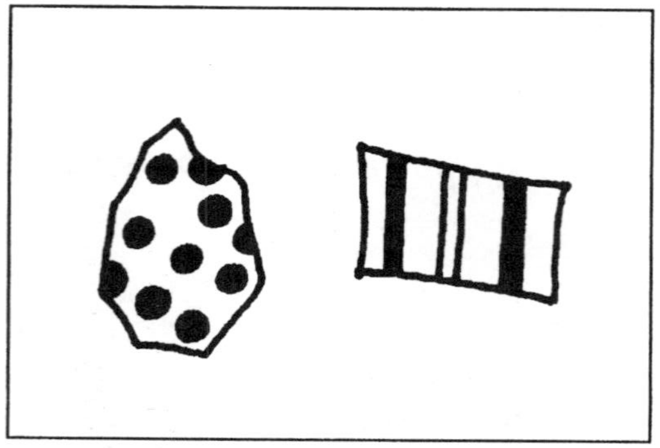

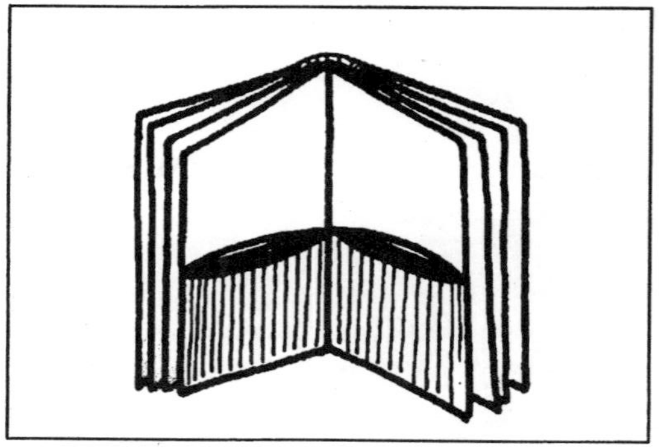

Activity Assessment Card

Name_____
Activity_____
Date_____

1. Level of Interest:

Pleasurable   Negative   Ho-Hum

2. Participation:

All Myself   Needed Help   No

Total Physical Assist:_____
Physical and Verbal:_____
Verbal Only:_____

3. Communication:

Great Day   Not So Good   Usual Day

Choices:_____
_____

Do It Yourself_____
_____

Comments:_____
_____

BAKER'S CLAY
4 cups unsifted flour
1 1/2 cups water
1 cup salt

Place all the ingredients in a bowl and mix thoroughly with your hands. Add small amounts of water if the dough is too stiff. Knead the dough about 5 minutes. After completing your project, place it on a cookie sheet and then into a preheated 350 degree oven. Bake for an hour (or longer if the project is thicker). Insert a toothpick and if it comes out clean, the project is done. Remove the project from the cookie sheet and allow it to cool on a rack. When completely cooled, the project may be decorated. Spray it with a clear fixative to preserve it.

Do not halve or double the recipe.
Use the dough within 4 hours.
Do not eat!

Appendix D

Discrepancy Analysis with Hypothesis

Directions for Discrepancy Analysis with Hypothesis

The Discrepancy Analysis with Hypothesis form is a four-step process whereby one may assess needed adaptations and skills for instruction. First, select an environment and an activity for instruction. Second, observe same-age peers performing the activity to identify the activity and the related skills necessary to independently participate in the activity. Third, identify how the individual with autism presently does the activity compared to typical peers. Lastly, determine what leisure activity or related skills will require instruction and/or adaptations.

For more information on the Discrepancy Analysis with Hypothesis and for an example of a finished form, see Chapter 6.

DISCREPANCY ANALYSIS WITH ADAPTATION HYPOTHESES

Student:		Age:		Date:	
Activity:		Environment:			
Subenvironments:					

Area	Skill	Competence	Adaptation
ID TIME			
RESOURCES			
CHOICE			
INITIATE			
SKILLS			
INTERACT			
PROB SOLVE			

References

The following references were reviewed in developing this book and may be of interest to the reader.

Bambara, L.M., P. Spiegel-McGill, R.E. Shores, and J.J. Fox. 1984. A comparison of reactive and nonreactive toys on severely handicapped children's manipulative play. *Journal of the Association for Persons with Severe Handicaps* 9 (2): 142-149.

Certo, N.J., S.J. Schleien, and D. Hunter. 1983. An ecological assessment inventory to facilitate community recreation participation by severely disabled individuals. *Therapeutic Recreation Journal* 17 (3): 29-38.

Coyne, P. 1980. *Well-being for mentally retarded adolescents: a social, leisure, and nutrition education program.* Portland: Oregon Health Sciences University.

Dattilo, J. 1986. Computerized assessment of preference for severely handicapped individuals. *Journal of Applied Behavior Analysis* 19 (4): 445-448.

———. 1990. Recreation and leisure: A review of the literature and recommendations for future directions. In *Critical issues in the lives of people with severe disabilities*, ed. L.M. Meyer, C.A. Peck and L. Brown, 126-137. Baltimore: Paul H. Brookes.

Dattilo, J., and P. Mirenda. 1987. An application of a leisure preference assessment protocol for persons with severe handicaps. *Journal of the Association for Persons with Severe Handicaps* 12 (4): 306-311.

Dattilo, J., and F. Rusch. 1985. Effects of choice on leisure participation for persons with severe handicaps. *Journal of the Association for Persons with Severe Handicaps* 10: 194-9.

Davis, D. 1993. Issues in the development of a recreational program for autistic individuals with severe cognitive and behavioral disorders. In *Handbook of autism and pervasive developmental disorders*, ed. D. Cohen and A. Donnellan, 371-383. New York: Teacher's Press.

Falco, R., and others. 1988. *Project quest inservice manual.* Portland OR: Portland State University.

Ferguson, D., and others. 1988. *The elementary/secondary system: supportive education for students with severe handicaps. Module 1: The Activity-Based IEP.* Eugene OR: University of Oregon, Specialized Training Program.

Ferguson, D., L. Jeanchild, and A. Todd. 1991. *The elementary/secondary system: supportive education for students with severe handicaps. Module 1a: The Activity-Based IEP.* Eugene OR: University of Oregon, Specialized Training Program.

Ferguson, D., and G. Meyer. 1991. *The elementary/secondary system: supportive education for students with severe handicaps. Module 1c: Ecological assessment.* Eugene OR: University of Oregon, Specialized Training Program.

Ferrara, C., and S.D. Hill. 1980. The responsiveness of autistic children to the predictability of social and non-social toys. *Journal of Autism and Developmental Disorders* 10 (1): 51-57.

Ford, A., and others. 1984. Strategies for developing individual recreation/leisure plans for adolescent and young severely handicapped students. In *Public school integration of severely handicapped students: Rational issues and progressive alternatives,* ed. N. Certo, N. Haring, and R York, 245-275. Baltimore: Paul H. Brookes.

Frith, U. 1989. *Autism: explaining the enigma.* Cambridge MA: Blackwell.

Gray, C., and C. Garand. 1993. Social stories: Improving responses of students with autism with accurate social information. *Focus on Autistic Behavior* 8:1-10.

Gutierrez-Griep, R. 1984. Student preference of sensory reinforcers. *Education and Training of the Mentally Retarded* 19:108-113.

Henning, J., and others. 1982. *Teaching social and leisure skills to youth with autism.* Bloomington IN: Indiana University Developmental Training Center.

Henning, J., and N. Dalrymple. 1986. *A guide to developing social and leisure programs for students with autism. In Social behavior in autism,* ed. E. Schopler and G. Mesibov, 321-349. New York: Plenum.

Howe-Murphy, R., and B.G. Charboneau. 1987. *Therapeutic recreation intervention: An ecological perspective.* Englewood Cliffs NJ: Prentice-Hall.

Joswiak, Kenneth F. 1989. *Leisure Education.* Venture Publications.

Lewis, V., and J. Boucher. 1995. Generativity in the play of young people with autism. *Journal of Autism and Developmental Disorders* 25 (2): 105-120.

McHale, S.M. 1983. Social interactions of autistic and nonhandicapped children during free play. *American Journal of Orthopsychiatry* 53: 81-91.

Mesibov, G.B. 1991. Learning styles of students with autism. *The Advocate Winter.*

Nietupski, J., S. Hamre-Nietupski, and B. Ayres. 1984. Review of task analytic leisure skill training efforts: Practitioner implications and future research needs. *Journal of the Association for Persons with Severe Handicaps* 9 (2): 88-97.

Realon, R.E., J.E. Favell, and J.F. Phillips. 1989. Adapted leisure materials vs. standard leisure materials: evaluating several aspects of programming for profoundly handicapped persons. *Education and Training in Mental Retardation* 24 (2): 168-176.

Realon, R.E., J.E. Favell, and K.A. Dayvault. 1988. Evaluating the use of adapted leisure materials on the engagement of persons who are profoundly, multiply handicapped. *Education and Training in Mental Retardation* 23 (3): 228-237.

Riguet, C.B., and others. 1981. Symbolic play in autistic, down's, and normal children of equivalent mental age. *Journal of Autism and Developmental Disorders* 11 (4): 439-449.

Schleien, S. J. (editor), et al. 1994. *Lifelong Leisure Skills and Lifestyles for Persons With Developmental Disabilities.*

Schleien, S.J., and M.T. Ray. 1988. *Community recreation and persons with disabilities: strategies for instruction.* Baltimore: Paul H. Brookes.

Strahmer, A.C. 1995. Teaching symbolic play skills to children with autism using pivotal response training. *Journal of Autism and Developmental Disorders* 11 (4): 123-141.

Tedrick, Ted (editor). 1997. *Older Adults With Developmental Disabilities and Leisure: Issue, Policy, and Practice.*

Uline, C. 1982. Teaching autistic children to play: A major teacher intervention. In *Teaching and mainstreaming autistic children,* ed. P. Knoblock. Denver: Love.

Voeltz, L.M., B.B. Wuerch, and B. Wilcox. 1982. Leisure and recreation: preparation for independence, integration, and self-fulfillment. In *Design of high school programs for severely handicapped students,* ed. B. Wilcox and G.T. Bellamy. Baltimore: Paul H. Brookes.

Wacker, D.P., and others. 1985. Evaluation of reinforcer preferences for profoundly handicapped students. *Journal of Applied Behavior Analysis* 18: 173-178.

Walker. 1990. *Resources on Integrated Recreation Leisure Opportunities for Children and Teens With Developmental Disabilities.*

Walker, P., and others. 1988. *Beyond the classroom: involving students with disabilities in extracurricular activities at levy middle school.* Syracuse NY: Center of Human Policy.

Watters, R.G., and D.E. Wood. 1983. Play and self-stimulatory behaviors of autistic and other severely dysfunctional children with different classes of toys. *Journal of Special Education* 17: 17-35.

Wehman, P. 1983. Recreation and leisure needs: a community integration approach. In *Autism in adolescents and adults,* ed. E. Schopler and G. Mesibov, 111-130. New York: Plenum.

Wehman, P., and M.S. Moon. 1985. Designing and implementing leisure programs for individuals with severe handicaps. In *Integrating moderately and severely handicapped learners*. Springfield IL: Charles C. Thomas.

Wehman, P., and S.J. Schleien. 1981. *Leisure programs for handicapped persons*. Baltimore: University Park Press.

Wehman, P., S.J. Schleien, and J. Kiernan. 1980. Age appropriate recreation programs for severely handicapped youth and adults. *Journal of the Association for the Severely Handicapped* 5: 395-407.

Wilcox, B., and G. Bellamy. 1987. *The activities catalog: an alternative curriculum for youth and adults with severe disabilities*. Baltimore: Paul H. Brookes.

Wuerch, B.B., and L. Voeltz. 1982. *Longitudinal leisure skills for severely handicapped learners*. Baltimore: Paul H. Brookes.